The Cornwall gardens guide

by
Douglas Ellory Pett

With additional research by
Margaret Grose

and a foreword by
Sir Richard Carew Pole

President of the Cornwall Gardens Trust

Alison Hodge

Published in 2006 by
Alison Hodge
Bosulval, Newmill, Penzance, Cornwall TR20 8XA
info@alison-hodge.co.uk www.alison-hodge.co.uk

First published 2003
This edition 2006

2nd revised edition ISBN 13 978 0 906720 48 6
                     ISBN 10 0 906720 48 6
(First edition 0 906720 32 X)

British Library Cataloguing-in-Publication Data
A catalogue record for this book is available from the
British Library.

Designed by Christopher Laughton
Originated by BDP – Book Development & Production,
Penzance, Cornwall
Printed in Singapore

Contents

Foreword by Sir Richard Carew Pole, President of the Cornwall Gardens Trust

Nothing gives me more pleasure than to write the Foreword for this splendid Guidebook. Cornish garden-owners have made a tremendous contribution to the history of gardening in this country. Throughout the 19th and 20th centuries, gardens have been developed in Cornwall by imaginative and creative owners, some of whom have been plant-hunters, or have supported others in their search for unusual plants in some of the world's remotest parts. This generation can now benefit from seeing mature plants and trees collected by these early expeditions growing and flourishing in our unique climate.

Cornwall is well known for its wide diversity of gardens, and Douglas Pett must be congratulated on putting together this book, which will provide guidance and inspiration for all garden-lovers wherever they may come from.

Richard Carew Pole
Antony House, Torpoint

4

The Cornwall Gardens Guide is the most comprehensive guide to the gardens of Cornwall. It includes over 130 gardens, public and country parks that open regularly, and a supplementary list of significant historic gardens that are accessible only occasionally.

For each garden there are map references, road directions, and full details for enquiries. Typical opening times and facilities are listed, and the pronunciation of Cornish place-names – often puzzling to visitors – is explained. English Heritage gradings in their Register of buildings and artifacts, and in the Register of gardens, as well as national and local designations for landscape beauty are included, to indicate those places officially recognized – although this in no way suggests that many other gardens are not equally, and in some cases more worth visiting.

Practical gardeners will welcome the notes for each of the main gardens on size, altitude, aspect, average rainfall and temperature, and soil – each of which affects the growth of plants.

The Guide is lavishly illustrated with photographs of the location and special features of the gardens, and specimens of individual flowers, many of which are characteristic of the local climate, and some (like those on Tresco, to the right) rarely seen in the open elsewhere.

The Introduction looks at the geology and climate of the region, and at the development of horticulture and design through the ages, especially in relation to Cornish gardens.

Further information about the wealth of historic gardens in Cornwall may be found in the definitive *The Parks and Gardens of Cornwall*,[1] which is illustrated with historic prints and contains detailed references. A number of contemporary gardens in Cornwall, and how they were made, are described more fully in *Creative Gardeners*.[2] Plant-lovers are referred to W. Arnold-Forster's classic *Shrubs for the Milder Counties*,[3] and Philip McMillan Browse's *Gardening on the Edge*,[4] which describes present-day experiences.

Douglas Ellory Pett
March 2003, revised 2006

1 Pett, D.E., 1998, *The Parks and Gardens of Cornwall*, Alison Hodge.
2 Pett, D.E., 2005, *Creative Gardeners*, Alison Hodge.
3 Arnold-Forster, W., 2000, *Shrubs for the Milder Counties*, 2nd edn, Alison Hodge.
4 McMillan Browse, P. (ed.), 2004, *Gardening on the Edge*, Alison Hodge.

Preface

The first impression of a visitor to Cornwall is that it is quite un-English. Crossing the bridge over the Tamar at once induces a sense of isolation. Here are no large towns, such as Plymouth or Exeter. Villages are scattered, clustering around crossroads, or along a highway, often with the church standing apart. The windswept plateaux, out of which rise great granite bosses, are covered with a tapestry of small, squarish fields, surrounded by stone- or slate-walled hedges, dotted at surprisingly regular intervals with isolated farmsteads. Everywhere are the relics of antiquity, and the wastes of mining and quarrying.

Introduction

Out of this historic landscape sprang up the manor houses and mansions, set in luxuriant gardens and parks, which were influenced by, and utilized the unique features of the terrain. Before looking at the history of these estates, we shall examine briefly the physical characteristics that moulded their shape.

Geology and soil

Cornwall forms the western projection of 'Highland Britain'. The peninsula runs in a south-west – north-east direction, narrowing from about 50 miles (80km) at its widest point in the east, to an average of 20 miles (32km), with most of the region within five to eight miles (8–13km) of the coast or a tidal estuary, thus everywhere experiencing a more or less maritime climate.

The underlying formations are of two kinds – granite, or 'killas' (the country rock). The soil over the granite is typically peaty and acid, so by choice very few of the gardens are found there. Where the granite thrusts through the killas, the rock became heated and created changed – 'metamorphic' – forms, and it was in these regions that minerals were deposited that brought wealth to the great mining areas of St Just, Camborne–Redruth and Callington.

Around St Austell the granite decayed into china clay, which was of equal economic importance, leading to the growth of a prosperous town where, during the 18th and 19th centuries, many new gardens were created.

However, not all of the killas was fertile. Along the north coast it produced a sticky clay which, combined with strong winds was not conducive to horticulture, so here mansions are thin on the ground. To the south, the serpentines of the Lizard peninsula formed another area where the soil is unfavorable to cultivation, only **Bonython** (5) and **Trelowarren** (29), which lie off the serpentine, being successful.

The highest quality soils are found in three areas: in the west, a triangle running from Lelant to Perranuthnoe and Penzance, which encompasses the gardens of **Trewidden** (33), Trengwainton (30; photo page 7) and **Trevarno** (32); in the east, the slopes of the Tamar Valley, between Callington and Saltash, are the site for **Cotehele** (102), **Pentillie Castle** (127), **Antony** (99) and **Ince Castle** (108); but it is in the central area, along the western side of the Fal estuary up to Truro, that the highest density of Cornish gardens is found, among them **Carclew** (121), the three Fox gardens, and the oldest estate of all – **Enys** (41). Even so, it was as much the topography as the soil that led to their success. **Trebah** (58) and **Glendurgan** (43), as well as **Bosahan** (6) and other gardens on the Helford estuary are all 'ravine' or valley gardens. So it is no surprise that in the valleys of the Fowey and Looe rivers there are similar concentrations; indeed, it is the estuaries that embrace the majority of the more celebrated parks and gardens in Cornwall.

Climate

For the horticulturist, climate is an inexact science, since every garden has its own frost-pockets and hot-spots. However, there are trends that make the weather in Cornwall unusual, if not unique.

Rainfall and humidity

Rainfall is on average some ten inches (25.5cm) less than on Dartmoor, Wales and other similar areas, and closely reflects the topography, rising towards the higher moorland, with the driest areas along the north coast. Perhaps of equal importance for the growth of plants is the humidity, which in Cornwall is unusually high, averaging around 80 per cent. This is welcomed by species such as camellias, rhododendrons and conifers, for which Cornwall is celebrated, but causes frustrating damping off in other varieties that originate in drier climes.

Temperature

The climate of Cornwall is warmer and more equable than anywhere else in Britain, but this is commonly misunderstood by those with little experience of gardening here. The frequent use of the expression 'sub-tropical' conjures up an imaginary land of hot summers and frost-free winters, where bananas and date palms flourish. A glance at a temperature chart will at once dispel any such illusions. 'Equable' signifies a climate that has a narrow range between its high and low average temperatures, which in Cornwall is the narrowest in the country. Frosts are infrequent, but it is never very hot in summer. This has important consequences for vegetation, for although for much of the year the temperature does not fall below that required for growth, it is seldom hot enough to provide the roasting needed by some quite hardy plants to ripen and flower.

However, it is probably the lower end of the scale, and especially the occasional extremes that are of most interest to the Cornish gardener who experiments with plants on the margin of hardiness. Whereas rainfall rises over the higher ground, temperature falls. Exceptionally, temperatures of -8°C may be experienced even in the warmest places, and from -10° to -12°C on the Devon border. These figures are 'means' – mid-points – reduced to mean sea level, which fall lower as the ground rises.

In general terms, the procession of seasons in Cornwall differs from that in other parts of the country: spring arrives early, summer late; autumn is long and winter short. In such a climate, even though relatively frost-free, it is the unexpected early or late frost that causes the greatest havoc.

Wind

As long ago as the 16th century, Norden described the 'fierce & furious wyndes' that 'sharply assayl the naked hills & dales', and nothing has changed. Although no-one escapes, the exposed areas of the extreme west, the Lizard and the north coast suffer most. So from the earliest days the wise Cornishman has sought the shelter of a valley, or a south-east facing slope, with the protection of a screen of trees.

Garden history

The beginnings

The remains of the Iron Age 'courtyard houses' at Chysauster, near Penzance, each of which has an enclosure that may have been cultivated, are a good starting point for the history of gardening in Cornwall. They were followed by typical early or 'Celtic' settlements – usually solitary farmsteads, or at most small groups of farms, each with a 'close' attached.

In the 12th century, one of the contributions of the Normans was the impaling of nine deer parks, five of which were associated with their castles. Well over 100 deer parks are recorded in Cornwall, which eventually inspired the greater estates to surround their dwellings with parkland. Of these, **Boconnoc** (68; plan above) alone among these ancient parks has survived, the other deer parks being reduced to two only, at **Prideaux Place** (90) and **Tregothnan** (60).

The medieval period

As times became wilder, many felt the need to provide themselves with protection from marauders. Wealthier residents fortified their dwellings by castellating their houses, building towers, and walling-in their courtyards, perhaps with a gate-house or barbican at the entrance. No complete house of this type survives, but there are enough relics and illustrations to obtain a fair impression of how they might once have appeared. **Cotehele** (102) is the finest example, although it has undergone many alterations. The tower houses at **Boconnoc** (68) and **Godolphin** (12) have been completely replaced, and at **Pengersick** (16) little remains but the tower.

The 16th century

During the reign of Elizabeth I, the country was more settled and peaceful, and there was no longer any pressing need to fortify houses. As early as 1547, for instance, Sir Richard Edgcumbe's new house at **Mount Edgcumbe** (112), although castellated, was open and outward-looking. Nevertheless, a fashion for castles had taken root: the square brick **Ince Castle** (108; photo page 9), a century later, being the first in a long line of pseudo-castles and castellated houses.

Even without fortifications, however, the former pattern of living continued. Typically there would still be a walled forecourt, perhaps with a gatehouse. The various other courtyards fulfilled many functions – a 'green court' where a visitor could 'park' his horse, or a 'herbary' where pot-herbs, salads and green vegetables were grown. There might be fruit, bee or hop gardens too. Remnants of these courtyard gardens have survived here and there, but **Penheale Manor** (114) with inner, front and two side courts is the most intact. Its raised walk, and possible relics of fish ponds add elements essential in the greater houses.

The 17th and 18th centuries

The Restoration after the Commonwealth marked a watershed in garden design, after which landowners were able to build on a more lavish scale, often with elaborate formal gardens in the Dutch or Italian manner. Such a garden at **Trebartha** (117), quartered, with slender trees at each corner, and statues both in each quarter and in the centre, is illustrated in the manuscript *Spoure Book* of *c.*1690. In the early 18th century, Edmund Prideaux left a finer collection of sketches made during two tours in 1716 and 1727, mostly to houses of his relatives, which show similar elaborate designs at his own **Prideaux Place** (90), **Antony** (99) and other houses. Today, the magnificent Italian and French gardens at **Mount Edgcumbe** (112) alone remain to represent this era.

By the middle of the 18th century, all of these formal gardens were swept aside to make way for the new landscape style. The influence of William Kent, one of the first of these designers, was to be seen at **Werrington** (131), which was adorned with a triumphal arch, temples, a ruined castle, hermitage, and ornamental bridge, set in a landscape of clumped trees. 'Capability' Brown, however, never

ventured as far west as Cornwall, although his ideas were carried back by the aristocracy and gentry who travelled to London, or visited the estates of their fashionable relatives. Moving west, aside from **Mount Edgcumbe** (112), **Port Eliot** (128), **Boconnoc** (68), **Chyverton** (123), **Tehidy** (26) and Clowance (now in timeshares) were all influenced by this new landscape trend.

Towards the end of the 18th century, the political influence of the Pitt family, through their relatives at **Boconnoc** (68) and **Port Eliot** (128), introduced Humphry Repton to Cornwall, where he prepared Red Books for **Antony** (99), **Port Eliot** (128), **Catchfrench** (122) and **Trewarthenick** (130) after his visit in 1792, and for **Tregothnan** (60) and **Pentillie Castle** (127) visited in 1809. But as explained above, the terrain in Cornwall does not lend itself to this style of gardening, and the new century introduced new concepts more suited to the lie of the land.

The 19th and 20th centuries

Even though Repton continued to be active in the early years of the 19th century, it was John Claudius Loudon who was the more representative of the new century, for he addressed a rising and prosperous middle class. He personally

(58; photo left), and emulated at **Heligan** (81) and many other gardens.

The thirst for new varieties continued throughout the 19th century. The brothers William and Thomas Lobb, whose father had worked at **Pencarrow** (86) and later at **Carclew** (121), were sent by Veitch's Exeter nursery to explore the American continents and the Far East. Mid-century, Joseph (later Sir Joseph) Hooker's Himalayan travels were introducing ever increasing numbers of rhododendrons – a species that had appeared in this country only in the first decade of the century. Their introduction inspired some of the more adventuresome among the gardeners to hybridize these new species. Samuel Smith at **Penjerrick** (52) and Richard Gill at **Tremough** (62; now a university campus developed as part of the Combined Universities in Cornwall) were the most notable of these.

The 'acclimatization of exotics' was another early enthusiasm. In 1837, George Croker Fox of Grove Hill, Falmouth, who had a reputation for growing oranges, lemons and bananas in the open, won the Banksian Medal of the Royal Horticultural Society of Cornwall for a list of newly introduced plants, while Augustus Smith at **Tresco** (1), encouraged by the unique climate on the Isles of Scilly, was beginning to grow pelargoniums, mesembryanthemums and agaves in the open.

The Royal Horticultural Society of Cornwall was founded in 1832, but had run out of steam by 1861. However, the inauguration of a Cornwall Daffodil and

visited four gardens in Cornwall: **Mount Edgcumbe** (112), **Pentillie Castle** (127), Tor House, and Trematon Castle, and included ten in the gazetteer in his *Encyclopoedia* of 1822, among which **Carclew** (121) perhaps reflected most clearly the new mood among garden-owners. Sir Charles Lemon, who then owned Carclew, was himself a correspondent of the botanists William and his son Joseph Hooker, whom he later sponsored in his Himalayan expedition, and it was on their recommendation that he appointed William Beattie Booth, with botanical skills, as his gardener.

As early as 1811 Worgan, in his survey of agriculture in Cornwall, had remarked on the increased planting of trees, but this was less in the open landscape than in the valleys, at first as windbreaks to protect the new species of trees and shrubs that were increasingly being introduced. Thus the 'valley garden' was to become the most characteristic of all the Cornish innovations. Of these the first, and perhaps the most influential, was **Penjerrick** (52), where it was the skill in the association of the various trees, as well as their range, that impressed contemporary horticultural writers. Robert Were Fox's example was followed by his brothers at **Glendurgan** (43) and **Trebah**

Spring Flower Society in 1867 by J.C. Williams of **Caerhays** (71), and his cousin P.D. Williams of Lanarth, arose from the new commercial sales of narcissus begun on the Isles of Scilly. The interest in daffodil-breeding was shared by George Johnstone of **Trewithen** (65) and others.

By the end of the 19th century, horticulture and the collection of vast numbers of plants had displaced the grand designs of the 18th century. J.C. Williams demonstrated his passion for new species by sponsoring first the expeditions of Wilson and Farrer in China and the Far East, and later those of Forrest. In this generosity he was joined by George Johnstone and, in the 20th century, Edward Bolitho of **Trengwainton** (30), in financing the journeys of Frank Kingdon Ward. The discoveries of new camellias and magnolias, as well as rhododendrons, inspired a new breed of hybridist – no longer practising gardeners, but enthusiastic owners. E.J.P. Magor, a solicitor, at **Lamellen** (125) was among the earliest of these, followed by E.G.W. Harrison, a retired General, at the nearby Tremeer, both of whom were in the forefront of rhododendron breeders; while at **Tregrehan** (95), Gillian Carlyon produced new camellia crosses until her death in 1987.

The complacency of the Edwardian era was shattered by the onset of the First World War in 1914. Many estates never recovered from the depletion of their staff by mobilization and death, and later by the need for financial retrenchment. Great houses were sold off as hotels, schools or hospitals, and their estates split up or neglected.

In the second half of the 20th century, climate changes – probably cyclic, since complaints of 'unseasonable' weather were common enough in the previous century – brought high winds in December 1979 and January 1990, and freezing gales in January 1987, which ravaged the protective shelter in many gardens.

In the face of such adversities, it is perhaps surprising that so many of the great gardens have preserved at least some of their former beauty, and have even, as at **Trebah** (58), **Heligan** (81) and **Trevarno** (32), been revived. Some fine new gardens, such as **Pine Lodge** (87), **Lamorran** (49) and **Bosvigo** (39), have been created, but the future will probably lie more with the many new gardens of an acre or two, designed on a much smaller scale, which have been planted and are being maintained solely by their owners, often in retirement, and which are themselves evidence of changing social patterns and ambitions.

Times of opening

This Guide contains descriptions of over 120 gardens in Cornwall open at the time of publication, the majority of which have been, and may be expected to remain open for many years. A few smaller, private gardens, open for only a day or two annually, may change from year to year, when their owners, often retired or elderly, move or find opening too exacting, so it is always advisable to check in advance current times of opening. For this purpose, contact telephone, email and web details are given. Information about gardens for which contact numbers are not given, or that have opened since this book was published, may be found in the 'yellow book', *Gardens of England and Wales Open for Charity*, of the National Garden Scheme (NGS), or on their website **www.ngs.org.uk**. Several of the gardens listed may open on additional occasions for charities or local events, which may

How to Use this Book

be advertised in the sources noted on page 266. Since hours of opening vary from year to year, opening times are given simply as 'am' (morning, usually from 10 a.m.) or 'pm' (afternoon, usually 2–5 p.m.), or 'am, pm' (morning and afternoon).

Please remember that most of the smaller gardens are private property, and are opened occasionally only through the generosity and enthusiasm of their owners. Do not assume that they can be entered at times other than those stated, or that on the larger estates a charity opening implies any public rights of way. When approached with consideration, most gardeners will be happy to share their experiences with you.

Finding a garden

The gardens are grouped into five regions (each with a short introduction), and arranged alphabetically within a region. For purposes of cross-reference, they are numbered sequentially throughout the Guide. For each entry, the name of the owner (who is not necessarily the person who will answer enquiries); the address; contact enquiry numbers, and road directions (given in miles [ml]) are provided. In addition, the pronunciation of Cornish names is shown by a phonetic spelling, with the stressed syllable in capital letters – usually the last in two-syllable, and next-but-last in longer names.

Each garden has a grid reference – which applies equally to the Ordnance Survey *Landranger* 1:50 000 (one inch to the mile), and *Explorer* 1:25 000 (two and a half inches to the mile) – for the square in which it is to be found and may be named. The first two figures refer to the left-hand side of the square, the second two figures to the bottom line. In order to help you plan a garden visit, a 1:550 000 (approx. one inch to nine miles) map is provided inside the back cover of the Guide. Permanent brown road signs show the way to major gardens, and temporary yellow signs indicate gardens open under the NGS.

Appreciation and official ratings

Where appropriate, garden descriptions give information about the history of the site and the persons who created the garden, so that the plants and features may be appreciated in a wider perspective.

Some properties have been graded by English Heritage (EH). In such cases, the **gradings** for the house and garden are given separately. There are three grades – I, II*, or II. Similarly, landscape **designa**

ns are given for the localities – AONB,
e national designation for an *Area of
Outstanding Natural Beauty* – and the two
cal designations – SAGLV for a *Special
Area of Great Landscape Value*, and AGLV
for an *Area of Great Landscape Value*.

ze, aspect, soil and climate

or most gardens, the aspect, climate,
il and size are given. Temperatures are
vided into zones, dependent upon the
erage minimum temperature in Febru-
y, the coldest month in Cornwall. They
e as follows:

A 5–4.5°C
B 4.5–4°C
C 4–3.5°C
D 3.5–3°C
E 3–2.5°C
F 2.5–2°C
G 2–1.5°C

ants

ost gardens that open have their own
ants for sale. These are distinguished
om larger nurseries as follows: **plant
entre** refers to a small 'nursery', such
s those in some National Trust gardens;
ursery signifies a commercial nursery
sociated with a garden, such as those
Bosvigo (39), **Pinsla** (88), and **Trewith-
n** (65). These may also be described as
pecialist' – such as the bamboo nursery
Carwinion (40) and the clematis and
elargonium nursery at **Roseland House**
1); 'wholesale'; or 'full-scale' – such as
Burncoose (7), one of Cornwall's pre-
ier nurseries. There is a full list of other
urseries, only some of which are associ-
ed with gardens, on pages 270–74.
   Some gardens listed have special plant
ollections registered by the National
ouncil for the Conservation of Plants
nd Gardens (NCCPG). These **National**

Collections are noted where they occur,
against the letters 'NC'.

Facilities

Facilities differ from garden to garden.
A key to the symbols used is given on the
flap inside the front cover. If a symbol
does not appear, the facility is not available – e.g., wheelchair access – or perhaps
not allowed – for example, dogs. However, enquiries may be made in special
cases. It is to be expected that guide dogs
for the blind will always be admitted.
A few National Trust gardens have a
Braille guide and scented gardens.

Historic gardens

A supplement of important **historic gardens** that open only occasionally (pages
266–9), gives suggestions for obtaining
information on opening times, which are
variable, or announced only locally.

Calendar

In order to find the gardens open at times
convenient to you, the **Calendar** (pages
275–7) groups them in three sections:

1 Open throughout the year
2 Open during the season
   – usually March to October
3 Open only on one or two
   days, arranged by months.

Each entry is cross-referenced to the
more detailed entries in the Guide.

Note

The information in the Guide is accurate
at the time of going to press. However,
gardens may change their hours of
opening, and neither the author nor
the publishers are responsible for any
such changes, which may occur without
notice.

The Isles of Scilly, although only some 28 miles out from Land's End, for most of their history led an isolated existence, often with little more than a subsistence economy. The mild, equable climate, usually frost-free, and rarely dropping below the 5°C necessary for the continual growth of vegetation, barely compensated for a landscape, never exceeding 45m (150ft) in altitude, barren of trees, quick-draining, short of natural supplies of water, and, except in a few places, not favoured with protection from the unceasing sea breezes.

The earliest settlement in historic times was an outpost of the Abbey of Tavistock on Tresco, which appears to have succumbed to marauders from the sea, to be replaced by a garrison on the island of St Mary's. The need to feed the military brought prosperity to the small population of inhabitants, but the peace following the end of the Napoleonic Wars led to a total collapse of the fragile economy, followed closely by famine. The Duchy of Cornwall, to whom the islands belong, were forced by public opinion to resolve the chronic poverty aggravated by the neglect of the Godolphins who were the leasehold 'Proprietors'. As a result, the lease was transferred to Augustus Smith, a young philanthropist from Ashlyns near Berkhamsted, who sought an opportunity to put his ideas into practice. His far-sighted, though despotic 'reign' was to earn him the title of 'Emperor of Scilly'. By the time of his arrival in 1834, it is probable that many exotic plants had already been introduced. The Hottentot Fig (*Carprobotus edulis*), and others – mesembryanthemums, echiums, and at least *Aeonium cuneatum* – all of which are now naturalized, most likely owe their introduction to passing sailors from the Mediterranean and Canary Islands. It was no doubt their attractiveness, and the potentiality of the unique climate that encouraged Augustus Smith to plant his own garden with tender species, once he

had decided to take up residence near the old Abbey on Tresco.

Later in the century, when the lucrative trade in early potatoes began to fail, on his suggestion, followed by William Trevillick at Rocky Hill on St Mary's, a box of the early daffodils found growing wild over the islands was sent to market with spectacular success. Some of these tazetta narcissi had been growing around the ruins of the Abbey, perhaps since the time of the monks, but the presence of 'Soleil d'Or', 'Grand Monarque' and *Narcissus biflorus* on The Garrison suggests that they may have been introduced by the soldiers' wives. 'Scilly Whites' were prolific in the orchards at Newford, the farm of the former Lord Proprietor's agent. The *Nar-*

1 ISLES OF SCILLY

issus 'Campernelli' had been given by the captain of a French ship to Mrs Gluyas, wife of the resident Dutch Vice-Consul and one of the early 'Pioneers', in the 1820s.

The narcissus trade was developed by Algernon Dorrien Smith, Augustus Smith's nephew and successor, who made a trial of over 350 varieties, some 240 of which he introduced from the Continent. From 1885 to the First World War, the market in daffodils soared, exciting regular comment in the horticultural press, so that for a time every available piece of land on the islands was cultivated. To protect the fragile blooms from the elements, they were grown in small fields with high hedges, at first of elm, escallonia,

tamarisk and veronica (*Hebe*). In the mid-1920s, resulting from the experience of his son, Arthur Algernon Dorrien Smith during his expeditions in the Antipodes, the use of pittosporum became virtually universal.

Today a visitor is immediately struck by the profusion of exotic plants seen even in modest front gardens – agaves and aloes; perhaps the tall mast of a flowering furcraea; the black form of *Aeonium arboreum* and the spicy, scented *A. balsamiferum*; the rounded bushes of *Geranium maderense*, with intense violet-purple flowers; the white daisy flowers of argyranthemums, and everywhere naturalized cinerarias. Unusual wild flowers abound in the fields and on the cliffs.

All year, am, pm

SV89 14; access by launch or helicopter regularly during summer season only

Robert Dorrien Smith

Tresco Abbey, Isles of Scilly TR24 0QQ

T: 01720 424105
F: 01720 422868
mikenelhams@tresco.co.uk
www.tresco.co.uk

TREsco

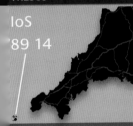

IoS
89 14

Gardens: I

6.9ha/17a

Lime-free

Sloping NNE–SSW, from 20m, in an AONB

76–89cm/30–35in

7.3–16.5°C

Acacias

Plant centre

The Tresco Abbey Gardens are unique in the British Isles for their display of exotic and tender plants. This has been made possible by exploiting the favourable maritime climate, where frosts are rare and usually not damaging, and the humidity is exceptionally high. The major destruction is caused by high or chilling winds, especially of long duration, which have required the planting of strong windbreaks of pine.

In 1838 Augustus Smith took up residence in the house he had built to his own design, perched on a rocky eminence above the Abbey ruins, looking out towards St Mary's, and at once began work on his garden, which by his death in 1872 had arrived at substantially the form in which it is seen today. He at first planted collections of pelargoniums and mesembryanthemums – or 'mesmerisms', as he called them – over 50 varieties of each, and later obtained plants from distant parts. His sister, Mrs Frances Marchant, a talented water-colourist, painted 51 sheaves of the many exotic flowers, which have been reproduced as postcards.

Augustus was succeeded by his nephew Thomas Algernon Dorrien, who adopted the name of Smith. Despite being at first inexperienced in horticulture, he applied himself to enhancing and extending the plantings, although he is perhaps better known for his work with daffodils. His son Arthur Algernon, who had botanized in Australia and New Zealand before taking over from his father in 1918, widened the range of plants from his contacts there and in South Africa.

1 The Abbey Gardens

Today the 'bottle-brush' flowers of grevillias and callistemons from the Antipodes, and the cone-shaped blooms of the proteas and leucanthemums from South Africa can be seen along the Top Terrace. The banks above the Middle Terrace are crowded with great American agaves – which astonished the first visitors to Tresco – and aloes, the smaller African equivalent, joined by the bizarre, almost horizontal, long red-stemmed flowers of the beschornerias, while everywhere are varieties of aeoniums endemic to the Canary Islands.

1 The Abbey Gardens (continued)

The icy gales of 1989 wreaked havoc in the garden, but most of the great cycads and some metrosideros trees miraculously survived or have regenerated. The damaged western end of the garden has been rejuvenated by a new, half-acre (0.2ha), Mediterranean Garden to a prize-winning design by Carey Duncan-Haouach. Other recent additions are sculptures of the children of Robert Dorrien Smith, and a Gaia by David Wynne.

open	At all times
directions	SV91 11, 1ml from Hugh Town along the Strand and Telegraph Rd; at a sharp bend take path straight ahead
owners	Community Garden
location	nr Longstone Terrace, St Mary's, IOS
enquiries	T: 01720 422404, or 01720 422153
pronounced	Crake Dew

IoS
SV91 11

size	0.6ha/1.5a
soil	Lime-free
altitude	30m, in an AONB
rainfall	76–89cm/30–35in
temperature	7–16°C

This community garden – the inspiration of June and Richard Lethbridge in 1986 – is planted and maintained largely by volunteers. It has been created on several levels in an old ram pit quarry – 'ram' being a local clayey earth used to make roads and paths. The garden is sheltered from damaging east winds, so that it is possible to grow a variety of sub-tropical plants, shrubs and trees. Among these will be found a palm – *Phoenix canariensis* – and cordylines, an albizia, *Acacia retinoides*, eucalyptus and the tree fern *Dicksonia antarctica*, as well as agaves and furcraeas. This is a tranquil spot, with seats to relax in peace and quiet to enjoy the flowering of multitudes of daffodils in the spring, pelargoniums in the summer, or belladonnas and nerines in the autumn.

2 Carreg Dhu

open	At all times
directions	In summer, daily launch services to the inhabited islands – St Mary's, St Agnes, St Martin's, Tresco and Bryher, and regular trips around the uninhabited islands
address	Isles of Scilly Tourist Information Centre, Hugh Town, St Mary's TR21 0LL
enquiries	T: 01720 422536 F: 01720 423782 E: tic@scilly.gov.uk www.simplyscilly.co.uk

IoS

Flowers abound everywhere – in front gardens; on roadsides; in fields, and in the wild. In the centre of Hugh Town, **St Mary's**, the little gardens of the houses around the Park are bright in summer with the day-glow colours of the mesembryanthemums, the succulent leaves of aeoniums, and the various coloured geraniums. A stroll around the Garrison passes large formal gardens, luxuriant with hydrangeas, hebes and phormiums; the cottagey garden of Veronica Lodge ablaze with tender plants, and informal wayside beds full of sub-tropical plants – the battery opposite Newman House glowing in summer with an unbelievable mantle of wild *Sedum acre*, lampranthus and cineraria, all self-sown. In the centre of the island, the favoured climate of Holy Vale, once celebrated for its produce, now sports phoenix palms, trachycarpus and cordylines, with phormiums, echiums and furcraeas, as if on some Mediterranean shore.

On **Tresco**, the Island Hotel has a large garden, and there are woodlands. In the 'off' islands there is perhaps less formal cultivation, but so many of the more unusual plants, such as the aeoniums, echiums, lampranthus and 'mesems' have become naturalized that there is scarcely need for gardeners. The visitor may be surprised to find agapanthus, libertia, and the belladonna lily growing wild. *Gladiolus byzantinus*, known as 'Whistling Jacks', are common. There is no end to the wild flowers, but mention may be made of the old bulb fields where ixias – relics of former flower-crops – may still survive, among the striking golden corn marigold *Chrysanthemum segetum*, known locally as 'Bothams', and the tender succulent 'Bermuda buttercup' – *Oxalis pes-caprae*.

Penzance and St Ives

The landscape of the extreme west of Cornwall, and the old hundred of Penwith, already denuded of trees before historic times, is a patchwork of small, prehistoric or 'Celtic' fields, scarred by mining. Only in the valleys running down to the sea, such as **Trewoofe** (34, 35) at Lamorna, could the planting of trees and gardens be attempted successfully.

The principal fishing harbours grew up on the south coast at Mousehole and Newlyn, and on the north coast at St Ives, where in the narrow streets and alleys, 'the abominable stench' of pilchards once 'assailed the nostrils'. Here little gardens now glow over a long period with the vivid colours of mesembryanthemums, fuchsias and pelargoniums. Penzance eventually emerged as the main port and market centre, receiving its charter as a borough in 1614, and becoming the coinage town for assaying tin and copper in 1663. By the turn of the 19th century, when the Napoleonic wars had made overseas travel impossible, the borough, with its exceptionally mild climate, took on a new lease of life as 'the Montpellier of England', becoming prosperous enough for rich merchants and lawyers to build handsome villas such as **Morrab** (14) and **Penlee** (17) in town, or to erect their mansions, like the Bolithos at **Trengwainton** (30) and **Trewidden** (33), higher up around the perimeter, facing the sea, and typically orientated towards **St Michael's Mount** (24).

(See gardens 4, 9, 10, 14, 17, 23, 24, 27, 30, 31, 33, 34, 35, 36, 37.)

Hayle and Helston

Hayle, not unreasonably, has been described as the 'cradle of the industrial revolution'. In the 1750s a number of adventurers from the Camborne district broke the monopoly of the Welsh smelting interests by setting up a Cornish Copper Company, which operated successfully until 1819, when it converted to an iron foundry. Of Hayle in those days a

contemporary wrote that as a consequence of

the fumes arising from the furnaces of Copper-house ... the glass placed in the windows of the habitations, after a little while loses nearly all its transparency. No bees can live within the polluted atmosphere, and in the gardens many valuable vegetables will not thrive.

With such an unsalubrious atmosphere, it is hardly surprising that the town attracted few wealthy residents.

Helston, in the hinterland of the Lizard, was granted its charter in 1201, at a time

Penzance
St Ives
Hayle
Helston
Camborne
Redruth

2 WEST

when the river Cober – cut off by the growth of Loe Bar in the 13th century - was still navigable. In these early days, Helston had no rival in the west nearer han Truro. The ancient estates of **Bony-hon** (5), **Godolphin** (12), **Penrose** (18) and **Trelowarren** (29), however, were situated at some distance from the town, and it was not until the 19th century that the prosperous citizens began to build villas such as Lismore, along the fashionable Cross Street.

(See gardens 5, 6, 8, 11, 12, 13, 15, 16, 18, 19, 20, 22, 29, 32.)

Camborne and Redruth

The Camborne and Redruth area, in the eastern section of the ancient hundred of Penwith, and on the granite of the Carnmenellis extrusion, lies open on the north coast to the Atlantic Ocean. This part of Cornwall was one of the richest in mineral resources, and was consequently the most extensively mined district in Cornwall. It is no surprise that all of the great houses here, such as those of the Bassets at **Tehidy** (26) and the Williamses at **Burncoose** (7), **Scorrier** (25) and **Treg-ullow** (28), arose out of their profits in the mining industry.

(See gardens 7, 21, 25, 26, 28.)

open	Apr–Oct, daily am, pm; Nov–Mar, Tues–Sun am, pm
owner	Tate St Ives
address	Trewyn Studio, Barnoon Hill, St Ives TR26 1AD
enquiries	T: 01736 796226 F: 01736 794480 E: tatestivesinfo@tate.org.uk www.tate.org.uk/stives

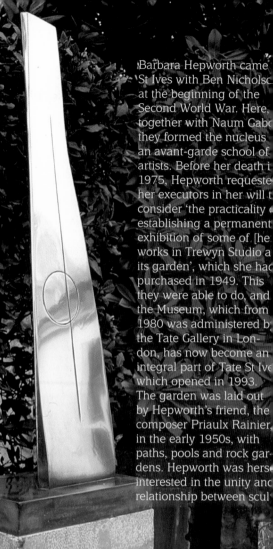

WEST

SX08 63

size	Very small
soil	Lime-free
rainfall	114–127cm/45–50in
temperature	Zone C

Barbara Hepworth came St Ives with Ben Nicholso at the beginning of the Second World War. Here, together with Naum Gab they formed the nucleus an avant-garde school of artists. Before her death i 1975, Hepworth requeste her executors in her will t consider 'the practicality establishing a permanent exhibition of some of [he works in Trewyn Studio a its garden', which she had purchased in 1949. This they were able to do, and the Museum, which from 1980 was administered b the Tate Gallery in London, has now become an integral part of Tate St Iv which opened in 1993. The garden was laid out by Hepworth's friend, the composer Priaulx Rainier, in the early 1950s, with paths, pools and rock gardens. Hepworth was hers interested in the unity and relationship between scul

e and its context. e, in this tiny garden ong palm, myrtle d cherry trees, camel- and ceanothus, we e the rare opportu- of seeing the works his great artist in just manner and setting which she herself shed to place them. The close-by **Trewyn** dens (below left), e part of the gar- of Trewyn House, ow a public park, nted with tender es and shrubs, and ourful bedding emes. A sculpture *egalith*, by John lne, was placed in gardens in 1976 as memorial to Barbara pworth.

4 Barbara Hepworth Museum & Sculpture Garden

open	mid-Apr–mid-Sep, Tues–Fri am, pm
directions	SW69 21, 5ml S of Helston on main A3083 Helston to Lizard road, turn L at Cury Cross Lanes by the Wheel Inn, entrance 300yd on R
owners	Mr & Mrs Richard Nathan
address	Bonython Manor, Cury Cross Lanes, Helston TR12 7BA
enquiries	T: 01326 240550 F: 01326 240478 E: sue@bonython manor.co.uk www.bonythonmanor .co.uk
pronounced	boNITHon, with a long 'i'
EH	House: II*

WEST

SX69 21

size	8ha/20a
soil	Alkaline and lime
altitude	75–60m
aspect	S-sloping, in an AONB
rainfall	89–102cm/35–40in
temperature	Zone B
	Plant sales

The estate dates back to the 13th century, but the fine main front of the present house was built in the 1780s, possibly to the design of William Wood, a pupil of Thomas Edwards of Greenwich. The house was described in the 19th century as being 'surrounded by considerable thriving plantations'. The which consist mainly of beech and Monterey pine, had been planted in the late 1830s by Treseder's nursery, the paths surfaced with pebbles from Loe Bar, near Helston. More recently, the main entrance drive was edged with lawns and blue hydrangeas, but since the arrival of the present owners from South Africa in 1999, considerable development ha taken place. The planting in the walled garden has been much extended by enlarging the herbaceous borders and creating a new, wide border between t swimming pool and lawn, with alliums rising abov a froth of catmint. A gate at the farther end leads into what was once the working area, now laid out as an elaborate potager, where the vegetables make a colourful display. Beyond, through the lower gate a vista opens up over a lightly planted orchard to Lake Joy, with an island and swans, and the countryside beyond. To the right of this lake, a second lake has been uncovered, which has been planted with ornamental grasses and tender South African species that have yet to mature. The new lake passes through a tree-fern and rhododendron dell, before emptying into a quarry pool, which is already picturesque, but will eventually be landscaped further. This formerly conventional garden has the potential to become one of the most interesting in the far west.

5 Bonython Manor

open	Mar–Sep, Mon–Fri am, pm, by appointment; groups by arrangement
directions	SW77 26, from Manaccan take road to St Anthony-in-Meneage. After 0.75ml turn L into drive by thatched lodge
owners	Mr & Mrs R. J. Graham-Vivian
address	Bosahan Estate Office, Manaccan, nr Helston TR12 6JL
enquiries	T: 01326 231351 F: 01326 231497 E: grahamvivian@ compuserve.com
pronounced	bosAIN

WEST
SW77 26

size	6ha/15a
soil	Lime-free
altitude	15m
aspect	N/E valleys, in an AONB, SAGLV
rainfall	102–114cm/40–45in
temperature	Zone B
	Plant sales

Bosahan is a garden of two valleys running down to the Helford River, the first of which is thought to have been planted in the 18th century. In the following century, the estate was developed by Sir Arthur Pendarves Vivian, who erected a large mansion – Bosahan Castle. He expanded the garden into two valleys and carried out extensive planting, so that Bosahan became one of the principal 19th-century valley gardens. It was described by P.D. Williams of Lanarth as 'one of the most happily chosen garden sites in Cornwall'. The species included specimen magnolias, numerous conifers, a large number of tree ferns, and the extraordinary number of 2,000 *Trachycarpus fortunei* palms. Much of this original planting survives. The garden contains about 250 mature species, and varieties from New Zealand, Australia, the Mediterranean area, South and Central America, and Asia. Massive podocarpus, cork oaks (*Quercus suber*), metasequoia, ginkgo, hoheria and eucryphia are among other specimen trees that have attained considerable dimensions in the favourable conditions. The present house (which is not open to the public), with its dramatic views to the river and sea, provides a smaller residence, while some walls of the old mansion have been incorporated into the gardens. Bosahan has an extensive, ongoing restoration programme, beginning with the cleaning and repair of the large pond, island and cascade. Besides traditional planting, recent work has introduced new varieties designed to extend interest over a longer season. The garden retains a special atmosphere, which the Graham-Vivian family is keen to preserve.

6 Bosahan

open	All year, excl 25 Dec, Mon–Sun am, pm
directions	SW74 39, 3ml SE of Redruth on A393 Falmouth road, 0.5ml beyond Lanner
owner	Mr C.H. Williams
address	Burncoose, Gwennap, Redruth TR16 6BJ
enquiries	T: 01209 860316 F: 01209 860011 E: burncoose@ eclipse.co.uk www.burncoose.co.uk
pronounced	burnCOOZe
EH	House: II

WEST

SW74 39

size	12.2ha/30a
soil	Lime-free
altitude	100–80m
aspect	S-sloping
rainfall	127–152cm/50–60in
temperature	Zone C
	Nursery: large, full-range, entrance free

The first of the houses built by the Williams family, after James Williams emigrated from Wales to Stithians, sometime before 1654. The garden was largely created between 1890 and 1916 by Mrs Powys Rogers, a daughter of J.M. Williams of **Caerhays** (71). Hamilton Davey, the Cornish botanist, described her as

> A genuine lover of gardening …
> For correctness in the massing of plants,
> Burncoose can be cited as an object-lesson,
> every plant introduced into the garden
> being placed in position with some definite
> object in view.

He also remarked on her collections of 'rare Alpin flora' and bamboos. The garden subsequently suffered neglect during the Second World War, and was damaged by a freak storm in December 1979. In 1984, however, the former Southdown Nursery which is now producing a vast range of ornament and exotic plants, moved here from Redruth to tak a central place on the estate, occupying the walled garden.

The private entrance to the property is now sep rated, rising from the lodge along a drive lined wi camellias, rhododendrons, and many other trees and shrubs. Further south, from this point edged with fine stone kerbs, it becomes one of the paths through the main plant collection to the west of th

Burncoose Garden & Nurseries

se, in front of
ch a lawn with
undial slopes
tly to a stone
ha. Beyond this is
ond surrounded
Japanese maples.
ng the perimeter
mature trees,
e 150 years
, including Holm
s. One of the
Monkey Puzzle
s is believed to
one of the tallest
ngland. *Mag-*
a spenderi diva
rncoose' and the
nellias 'Burncoose
le Blossom' and
nica Dance' were
ed here.

open	One Sun in Jun, and by appointment, pm
directions	SW72 24, between Mawgan and St Martin-in-Meneague. From Mawgan turn L into farm entrance after farm shop on R. From St Martin turn first R
owners	Louise McClary & Mathew Robinson
address	Caervallack Farm, St Martin, Helston TR12 6DF
enquiries	T: 01326 221339.
pronounced	carVALL'ck

P WEST

SW72 24

size	0.4ha/1.1a
soil	Lime-free clay
altitude	65m
aspect	In an AONB
rainfall	89–102cm/35–40in
temperature	Zone B
	Plant sales

An artist's garden, created by Louise – a painter and plant-lover – and her husband, Matthew – an architect – whose interests are reflected both in its structure and planting. The garden is better described as in compartments than 'rooms', since the are views as well as connecting links between the various parts. The entrance is through a roofed lyc type gate leading to the front of the house, facing open 'pump-house' attached to one of the thatchec cob walls that are a feature of this garden. From this point an old brick path forms the spine of the garden, at first straight through a pergola covered with wisteria, roses, and *Clematis armandii*, where the beds along the outside are planted with spheri mounds of box, underplanted with silver santolina Through the pergola to the left can be detected a formal courtyard garden with patterned paving an a central vase between four upright golden yews. A cob summerhouse backs on to the pump-house. To the right of the pergola, an informal gravelled area faces a large mixed bed. Emerging out of the pergola, the path weaves its serpentine way throug

variety of features. On one side, two metal lattice 'thrones' overlook a rectangular slate through which water bubbles, attended by a sculptured angel with bird. On the other side, 'beehive' pavilion looks upon a circular garden, with a tall metal fountain at the centre, whose mobile petals are operated by the flow of water. This little garden is enclosed on one side by a cob wall with gothick aperture and a serpentine tiled top, and on the other by a yew hedge. Entry is through the pavilion. This intriguing garden deserves to be seen to be appreciated.

8 Caervallack

open	Apr–Jun, Wed pm; Jul–Aug, Wed pm, Sun pm. Two weekends for NGS. Groups by appointment
directions	SW44 24, from Newlyn take B3315. Follow signs to Lamorna Cove Apartments, garden 200yd on L
owners	Dr & Mrs Robert Moule
address	Chygurno, Lamorna, Penzance TR19 6XH
enquiries	T: 01736 732153
pronounced	chyGURno

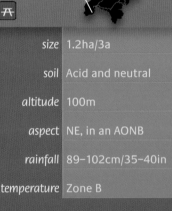

P **WEST**

SW44 24

size	1.2ha/3a
soil	Acid and neutral
altitude	100m
aspect	NE, in an AONB
rainfall	89–102cm/35–40in
temperature	Zone B

The rugged coastline and intense blue waters of Lamorna Cove form the backdrop to the dramatic cliffside garden at Chygurno. The house was originally built as a retreat for two suffragettes in 1908. Ler, the property lay unoccupied for 20 years, and th vegetation grew into an impenetrable mass. Since 1998, Robert and Carol Moule have set about carvi a maze of pathways and granite steps into the stee hillside, and work continues on opening up new areas. This is a young garden with a wealth of exot plants, many from the Southern hemisphere.

A particular glory is the collection of tree ferns, pla ed plentifully in glades and against rocky outcrops for heightened effect. There are several varieties, including *Cyathea dealbata*, the silver tree fern and national symbol of New Zealand. In sheltered positions, banana plants thrive, beside huge crinums, *Paulownia tomentosa*, and the Canary Island foxglove, *Isoplexis canariensis*. In late summer, numerous bees are attracted by flowering proteas – plants which, in common with almost all the species in th

…arden, remain outside all …rough the year. In the …igher garden, aeoniums …row vigorously and be-…ome a particularly intense …ark red. More brilliant …olour is provided by aga-…anthus and hydrangeas. …the early months of the …ear, a range of rhodo-…endrons, camellias and …zaleas come into their …wn, along with carpets of …uebells. A decked area …the house, supported by …ge timbers, juts out into …e garden and provides an …usual vantage point on …e-level with the treetops.

open	Two Suns a year, am, pm
directions	SW54 29, from Marazion take A394. Turn R to Perranuthnoe. 200yd on L take unmade lane
owners	Charles & Christine Taylor
address	Ednovean Farm, Perranuthnoe, Penzance TR20 9LZ
enquiries	T: 01736 711883
pronounced	EDnoVEAN

WEST

SW54 29

size	0.6ha/1.5a
soil	Lime and clay
altitude	80m
aspect	SW, in an AONB
rainfall	102–114cm/40–45in
temperature	Zone C
	Plant sales

Ednovean is a stone-built farmhouse converted from a 17th-century farm, situated on the rising ground behind Perranuthnoe and commanding extensive views over the countryside and across the wide sweep of Mount's Bay. A particular feature is the use made of views of the romantic outline of **St Michael's Mount** (24), here revealed by carefully shaped foliage, there framed by the doorways of a garden room, and in a little terrace unexpectedly revealed in a wall mirror. Around the house lie courtyards varying in size and character, each luxuriantly planted and providing sheltered seating. The main court is a sunken parterre, with small lawns surrounded by neat box hedging and a fountain at the centre. Terracotta pots and planters with clipped box add detail, while context is provided by date palms, figs and olive trees. On the seaward side a wide lawn, with cut-grass spiral and bordered by rich planting, leads to the Italian garden of long walks, enclosed spaces and constant surprises. Another pathway leads through a deep gravel border containing phormiums, palms, succulents, and feathery grasses. Hidden away is a secret patio garden, just big enough for a table and chairs, protected from th sea breezes and catching the best of the sun. Partic

lar attentio has been given to th planting of lavender and herbs, so that the scents are captured in the enclose spaces.
The garden has been created as an area of peace and relaxation, lulled by th sound of th distant sea

10 Ednovean Farm

open	Easter through Oct (closed some Mons and Fris in low season) – phone for opening times and prices
directions	SW67 26, from A394 follow official brown and white signs to Flambards, located on the A3083
owners	Mr & Mrs Douglas Kingsford Hale
address	Culdrose Manor, Helston TR13 0QA
enquiries	T: 01326 573404 F: 01326 573344 E: info@flambards.co.uk www.flambards.co.uk.

WEST

SW67 26

size	In 8ha/20a theme park
soil	Lime-free
altitude	70m
rainfall	102–114cm/40–45in
temperature	Zone B
	Plant centre

The greater proportion of Culdrose was absorbed into the Royal Naval Air Station, leaving a residue that was independently developed as the Flambards Village. At first this was little more than a theme park, but as new attractions were added so trees, shrubs and displays of flowers were planted to improve what had originally been a barren site of bog and scrub. It came to be viewed by the owners as no longer primarily a leisure centre, but more a 'garden containing various attractions'. The site was transformed – the various structures softened by the planting of flowers, and the different areas separated with large trees and shrub hedges, which introduced an element of surprise as visitors turned corners. The roller-coaster now emerges from swathes of hydrangeas and hebes, and the go-kart track is surrounded by slopes planted with shrubs. Hanging baskets overflowing with flowers abound, and Flambards has attracted many awards: the gardens have been voted 'Top Business Garden' by the local author-

11 The Flambards Experience

y for 15 years, including Best Hanging Baskets'. A theme park may not at first seem to hold appeal for the horticulturally minded, but then it is known that Flambards employs a head and even other gardeners, it is clear that the garden is no decline. The greenhouses contain exotic plants – orange and lemon trees, and banana plants, all of which produce fruit. The recently enlarged Plant Centre holds a large stock of plants and garden accessories.

open	Easter–Sep, Tue–Fri, Sun, and bank holiday Mons, am, pm; estate (NT) all year. Groups by appointment
directions	SW60 31, 1ml W of Helston on A394 to Penzance, turn R at Hilltop Garage on to B3302. After 1ml turn L to Godolphin Cross. House is 0.5ml on L
contact	Mrs Joanne Schofield
address	Godolphin House, Godolphin Cross, Helston, TR13 9RE
enquiries	T: 01736 763194 E: info@ godolphinhouse.com www.godolphin house.com
pronounced	g'DOLPHin
EH	House: I

WEST

SW60 31

EH	Gardens: II*
size	Garden, in large estate
soil	Acid
altitude	60m
aspect	Sloping NE, in an AGLV
rainfall	102–114cm/40–45in
temperature	Zone C
	Plant centre

42

In *c.* 1535, Leland reported that there were 'no grea Tynne Workes yn al Cornwall then be on Sir Wylliam Godalgan's Ground', and it was from the wealt of their mining that the power of the Godolphin family, and the grandeur of their estates, devolved. Leland visited Godolphin when Sir William was in the process of demolition, and of construction of hi new castellated north front, together with its avenu approach and new forecourt. The present north fron is a remarkable and in several respects unique design of the early Classicism of Charles I, dating from 1630.

The Side Garden to the east is an exceptional survival, a 'great garden' (4.5 acres/1.8ha) of 1500, one-third of which dates back to 1300. Wall-walks (part accessible) surround its nine compartments. Ponds lie on a terrace on the south, one dating from an Elizabethan reworking of the garden and one from about 1700, the work of Sir William 1V, a clos friend of John Evelyn. The earliest part of this garde is still gardened, the remainder being under grass. On Godolphin Hill, to the south, are remains of the deer park and warren of 1300.

Behind the stables, to the right of the house and accessed from within, is the 'King's Garden', named for a visit in 1646 of the future Charles II but, in fact, a privy garden of 1500. These two gardens are of national importance and have been the subject of extensive archaeological study as a prelude to restoration. It is a place of great intrinsic interest and atmosphere, often featured on television and in films. The wider Estate, with scenic walks over the former deer park, is now in the care of the National Trust.

12 Godolphin House & Estate

open	One NGS Sun pm in Apr and May. Groups by appointment
directions	SW77 24, 1ml out of centre of Manaccan village. Down hill past Inn on R, follow signpost to Carne. House on R, yellow NGS sign, park nearby
owners	Mr & Mrs Mark Osman
address	Hallowarren, Carne, Manaccan TR12 6HD
enquiries	See NGS yellow book, or www.ngs.org.uk.
pronounced	HALowarren

WEST

SW77 24

size	0.6ha/1.5a
soil	Lime-free
altitude	5m
aspect	In an AONB
rainfall	89–102cm/35–40in
temperature	Zone B

Set in a beautiful wooded valley bordering a stream. At its widest point, the house is surrounded by a cottage-style garden, where a pool opposite the house, fed by a stream, has been sown with candelabra primulas and other bog plants, to form a water garden. Among the surrounding trees are magnolias and a *Liriodendron tulipifera* – the tulip tree. The garden then rises up through the valley, where the grass walk is bordered with old roses, lilies and many unusual trees and shrubs. The impression created is that of a haven of cultivation snatched from wild nature.

Hallowarren has won first prize in the Kerrier Council Garden Competition for a Woodland or Shrub Garden (Southern Section) for several years. It has featured on West Country television, and in 2005 won second prize in the ITV West Country Garden of the Year competition. There is a walk through the adjoining woods, which are carpeted with bluebells in the spring.

13 Hallowarren

open	Daily, admission free, am, pm; Morrab Library, open to visitors, Tue–Fri am, pm; Sat am
directions	SW47 30; entrances from Morrab Road or from Promenade via St Mary's Road
owner	Penwith District Council
address	The Morrab Library, Morrab Road, Penzance TR18 4DA
enquiries	(Library) T/F: 01736 364474 www.morrablibrary.co.uk.
pronounced	MORrab
EH	House: II

WEST

SW47 30

EH	Gardens: II
size	1.4ha/3.5a
soil	Lime-free
aspect	S-facing
rainfall	102–114cm/40–45in
temperature	Zone C

Built in 1865–6 by Samuel Pidwell, a wealthy brew on open land running down to the sea, Morrab House passed eventually to Charles Campbell Ross banker who was MP for St Ives and four times May of Penzance. In the 1880s, when Penzance began extend, he moved to a site high above the town, a in 1889 the property was purchased by the Corpor tion for a municipal park, the house becoming the home of the Penzance Library. Reginald Upcher, a London landscape gardener, was engaged to lay o the grounds. His origin is somewhat obscure, but he may have been related to the Upchers of Sher- ringham Hall in Norfolk, a Repton garden. Whatev the virtues of his design, his knowledge of exotic plants appears to have been limited, and the reput tion gained by the Morrab Gardens in subsequent years owes more to the gardeners and park super- intendents than the original designer. By the early 20th century, Morrab Gardens were widely known their unique range of tender trees and shrubs, suc as eucalypts, myrtles, olives, and even bananas an oranges, many of which could not be grown in the open anywhere else in England, and fulfilling the prophecy of the *Gardeners' Chronicle* that

The new Penzance public park promises to give a great impetus to acclimatization ... where tourists may fancy themselves in the tropics or on the Mediterranean shores.

ere remains a Victorian ndstand, and a pool h a fountain, although e old cast-iron shelter s given way to more mfortable quarters for e aged. Despite the garies of the weather, d financial constraints, e Gardens have retained eir capacity to persuade sitors they have entered strange and unfamiliar orld.

14 Morrab Gardens

open	All year, daily, am, pm
directions	SW55 36, follow A30 to Hayle, from St Ives/ St Erth roundabout, then follow brown and white signs to Paradise Park
owner	Mr Michael Reynolds
address	Paradise Park, Hayle TR27 4HB
enquiries	T: 01736 751020 F: 01736 751028 E: info@ paradisepark.org.uk www.paradise park.org.uk

WEST

SW55 36

size	0.8ha/2a
soil	Alkaline
aspect	W-sloping, from 20m
rainfall	102–114cm/40–45in
temperature	Zone C
	Plant sales

Developed in the grounds of Glanmor, a Victorian villa built by a wealthy industrialist during the years of Hayle's prosperity, Paradise Park is a 14-acre (6ha) site, opened in 1973 as a breeding centre for rare and endangered birds. It has developed into a breeding collection of international importance, and is now the base for the World Parrot Trust. The former walled garden associated with the Victorian house has been utilized as a garden setting for exhibiting a selection of the more attractive and interesting birds. Here pergolas and trellis-work have been erected to support roses and clematis, with gazebos for a leisured view of the garden and birds. Three special features are 'Parrot Jungle', a walk-through 'Australian Aviary' and terraced 'Gazebo Garden' full of Southern hemisphere plants, including grasses. Paradise Park offers the opportunity to combine a garden visit with an enthralling exhibition of bird life.

15 Paradise Park

open	At any time by appointment
directions	SW58 28, turn off A394 at Germoe Cross Roads to Praa Sands. Pengersick is on R
owner	Mrs Angela Evans
address	Pengersick Castle, Praa Sands, Breage TR20 9SJ
enquiries	T: 01736 762579 F: 01736 763173 E: guyswordsman@ aol.com www.pengersickcastle. com
pronounced	penGERsick with a hard 'g'
EH	House: I

WEST

SW58 28

size	Small
soil	Lime-free
altitude	40m
aspect	In an AONB
rainfall	88–102cm/35–40in
temperature	Zone B

The description by Maton at the end of the 18th century, when Pengersick had long been a ruin, paints a more realistic picture of its condition down the centuries than is gained from its shape today.

> About four miles from Marazion, and a half an one from the high road, towards the coast, stands Pengerswick [sic] Castle, of which a square stone tower, of three stories, with a smaller one annexed, and some fragments of walls are the only remains. The door, on the north, is machicolated [through which hot coals could be dropped on invaders]. The different apartments are now used as granaries and hay-lofts, but the wainscoat, which is of oak, remains perfect. This wainscot is very curiously carved and painted, and there are several quaint pieces of poetry inscribed on the panels. A winding stone stair-case leads to the top of the principal tower, which commands a good view of the surrounding country.

Pengersick should be described as a fortified manor house, rather than a castle. It was built, probably at the end of the 15th century, for John Milliton, who was married to Elizabeth Worth, the last direct descendant of the Pengersick family who occupied the site from the 13th century. A sketch by William Borlase, when he visited in 1738, from the panelling described by Maton, gives a general impression of a typical tower-house with a walled front court. This court constitutes the present terraced garden, with a reconstructed archway leading to the original fortified domain of the Pengersick family. A garden trail has been created to trace the progress of cultivation from prehistoric to Tudor times, using archaeological evidence recently revealed. A link with the Wars of the Roses, the catalyst for the success of the Millitons, is now being illustrated with a display of 'Roses in the Context of History'. There is a 'Resource Centre' with information about the site, and the Tower may be visited. Pengersick is a Scheduled Ancient Monument.

16 Pengersick Castle

WEST

SW47 30

Land from the 'Lower Morrab' – a word which in Cornish meant the 'seashore' or seaward part of the parish – was conveyed to the prosperous miller, J.R. Branwell (of a Penzance family related to the mother of the Brontë sisters), between 1860 and 1865, after which he began to build his house, perhaps to the design of John Matthews, town surveyor for Penzance. Along the east side it had a conservatory, and was surrounded by parkland of a quite different style from that at the **Morrab Gardens** (14). After the Second World War, the property passed into the ownership of the Corporation as a Memorial. The entrance is through the garden beside the house, which is now a museum and art gallery. The walled garden has become the site of a small memorial chapel, framed with cordylines. The garden is laid out in small lawns, with beds containing a number of exotic species, such as the shrubby echium, and beschornerias. On the walls are various tender shrubs and climbers – fuchsias, bomarea, and *Asarina erubescens,* with the rare *Vallea stipularis* at the entrance. The parkland has been retained for the benefit of the public, chiefly as a recreation ground.

17 Penlee Memorial Gardens

open	Estate at all times to walkers; house and garden private
directions	SW64 25, access from 4 car-parks: (1) from Helston 1.25ml along Degibna Lane past Nansloe Manor Hotel; (2) 1.5ml from Helston along B3304; (3) and (4) both about 0.5ml along coast road E out of Porthleven
owner	NT
address	nr Helston
enquiries	T: 01326 561407 E: lizard@ nationaltrust.org.uk www.nationaltrust .org.uk.
pronounced	penROSE
EH	House, bath house: II

WEST

SW64 25

size	648ha/1,600a
soil	Lime-free
altitude	60m to sea
aspect	On NE-facing side of SE-sloping valley, in an AONB
rainfall	76–89cm/30–35in
temperature	Zone B

The Penrose family became extinct, and in 1770 the estate was sold to Hugh Rogers, whose brother John extended his lands, in 1785 establishing a deer park. The new owners added elegant stables with a clock turret, and relandscaped the grounds to take fuller advantage of the prospect over the Loe Pool and the Degibna Woods on the other side. A bath house was erected in about 1837 (restored by the National Trust), and some ten years later a bridge was built over the river, clearly intended to act as a feature in the view, which, as Pevsner remarked, overlooks 'Loe Pool as if it were an artificial serpentine lake especially made as a vista for the house'. It was at about this time that th Helston Lodge was constructed in a Victorian Tudo style, but the Bar Lodge, built in 1895–8 by estate workmen to designs of the Plymouth architect G.H Fellowes Prynne, was rather more elaborate, being adorned with a wooden balustraded balcony. This was intended to open into an impressive new drive up to the house, which was never completed.

John Jope Rogers, who lived at Penrose during the second half of the 19th century, had a lively interest in horticulture, and contributed several val able articles to journals, recording the effects upon trees and shrubs of the bad winters in 1860–61 an 1878–9. He also announced the fruiting of the uncommon *Abies religiosa* at Penrose – believed to have been the first time in this country.

The estate was the largest gift ever made to the National Trust in Cornwall.

18 Penrose

open	Apr–Aug, am, pm, by appointment only + donation to charity
directions	SW74 16, along Lizard road from Helston (A383), turn L on to B3293 to St Keverne. About 2ml after Goonhilly Earth Station, turn R immediately before the garage. Take 2nd turn R, signed to Gwenter, then 2nd turn L. Poldowrian is after Penhallick and Pensongath
owner	Mrs P.S. Hadley
address	Poldowrian, Coverack, Helston TR12 6SL
enquiries	T: 01326 280468 E: vjhadley@tiscali.co.uk
pronounced	polDOWrian

WEST

SW74 16

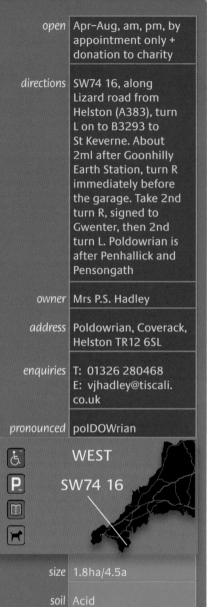

size	1.8ha/4.5a
soil	Acid
altitude	60m
aspect	S-sloping, in an AONB
rainfall	89–102cm/35–40in
temperature	Zone B

An almost indescribable wild garden along the very edge of the coast, not far from the southernmost point of the Lizard, Poldowrian has been created since 1969 along a narrow valley, where a stream runs down and over the cliff to the sea. Various pines – *Pinus radiata*, *P. muricata*, *P. contorta* and *P. maritima* – were planted to the west of the stream as a necessary windbreak against the gales. 'We have tried to make Poldowrian a blend of the wild and cultivated', the owner writes, adding, 'though the wild can quickly take over'! A pool was dug out early on at the top of the garden, and a small folly has been built on the island. The clematis, rhododendrons, camellias, cistus and ceanothus in the garden can be seen from the coastal path below. There are prehistoric sites here – the remains of a Bronze Age round house, and a probable Mesolithic workshop, radiocarbon-dated to 5500 BC – and the owner's Museum of Prehistory may be seen on request, making a visit to this garden a unique experience.

19 Poldowrian Garden

open	Apr~Sep, Sun, am, pm
directions	SW74 29, from Constantine take Falmouth road to High Cross, turn R to Port Navas, garden 100yd on R. From Treliever Cross roundabout on A39 nr Penryn for 3.5ml, take Mabe road past Argal reservoir to Lamanva crossroad, R to High Cross, L to Port Navas, garden on R
owners	Dan Thomas & Peter Skerrett
address	Potager Garden, High Cross, Constantine, Falmouth TR11 5RE
enquiries	T: 01326 341258 E: info@ potagergarden nursery.co.uk www.potagergarden nursery.co.uk
pronounced	'potajay', as in French

WEST

SW74 29

size	2ha/5a
soil	Lime-free
aspect	N-sloping from 95m, in an AONB
rainfall	102–114cm/40–45in
temperature	Zone C
	Plant sales

58

A visit to the Potager Garden will gain entry into the early stages of an innovative and – for Cornwall – a unique project in the process of development by a horticulturist and an architect. A 'potager' literally describes 'an ornamental productive garden', which is more usually seen as a parterre ornamented with colourful vegetables, with artificially trained fruit trees. Here, this garden is being designed along broader lines to demonstrate the beauty of productive gardening, both at the domestic level and in a wider perspective. The site had been used originally as a market garden producing flowers and fruit, but in the 1980s it became the 'High Cross Garden Centre'. This was taken over in 2000 for the Potager Garden, after many years of dereliction resulting in the invasion of bracken and bramble among overgrown trees. Great strides have been made in clearance, and in making a start with the project. The garden has been open for the Doubleday Foundation, and received Soil Association organic status in January 2004, both of which reflect the aspirations of the owners. Already students from the Falmouth School of Art attend for design sessions, in which they have created, among other projects, willow sculptures. A forge has been set up for metal work, and centres for craft and handmade furniture are up and running. Visitors will be encouraged not only to enjoy what they see, but also to learn how the ideas on conservation, energy-saving, and organic production are relevant and practical in their own gardens. This is an exciting new scheme set in a landscape that looks out over the Cornish countryside to distant hills.

20 Potager Garden

open	Apr–Sep, Tues and Wed, pm
directions	SW75 44, in Chacewater, at Truro end of main street
owners	Mr & Mrs C. Pridham
address	Roseland House, Chacewater, Truro TR4 8QB
enquiries	T: 01872 560451 E: clematis@ roselandhouse.co.uk www.roselandhouse. co.uk

SW75 44
WEST

size	0.4ha/1a
soil	Neutral
altitude	30m
aspect	SW
rainfall	102–114cm/40–45in
temperature	Zone C
NC	*Clematis viticella* cultivars
	Nursery specialist: clematis, pelargoniums, etc

The original house, dating from the 1700s, later passed to a mine captain, and was remodelled in 1847. Chacewater is in a mining area where the lig shaley soil conceals arsenic and mineral deposits t can prove lethal to plants that root into them. Whe the present owners arrived in the early 1980s, the garden was overgrown, so after clearing the groun they began to improve the soil, philosophically reconciling themselves to the loss of those plants that became poisoned. When Charlie Pridham reti from the Merchant Navy, he and his wife decided t supplement their income by starting a nursery. By this time, the pond in front of the house had been dug, and the leaning *Eucalyptus aggregata* planted which had been grown from seed. The beds behin the pond were then filled with an array of herba-ceous varieties, mixed with shrubs used principally as supports for a collection of some 300 climbers, roses and honeysuckles, and especially clematis, o which some 150 varieties are grown. A long pergo follows the path down the slope to the gate, over which climbs the deep pink *Clematis* 'Dr Ruppel', a the white 'Marie Boisselot'. There are also roses – t 'Kew Rambler', and the fragrant 'Mme Alfred Car-rière'. Sheltered in the greenhouse are scented-leaf pelargoniums, several varieties of passion flower, and a *Pandorea pandorana* 'Golden Rain'. The conservatory at the rear of the house, covered by *Wisteria floribunda*, contains the strongly scented *Jasminum polyanthum*, and the rose *R. chinensis* 'Mutabilis'. This upper garden contains some of the original trees, including old Cornish varieties – among them the 'Chacewater Long-stalk' apple, a curiosity that has fruits small enough to pass through the neck of a bottle, in which they would then be pickled.

21 Roseland House

WEST

SW79 20

size	8ha/20a
soil	Neutral to lime-free
aspect	NE-sloping from 90m, in an AONB
rainfall	76cm–102cm/30–40in
temperature	Zone B
	Plant sales

Tregellast Barton was first mentioned as early as 1311, and the farmhouse appears in the Tithe map of 1840. The Roskillys, a local family, came here in 1960 after the marriage of Joe Roskilly. Since then they have always supplied milk and cream, but like many other dairy farms have diversified. They have produced their well-known ice-cream since 1990, since when there have been many developments: a shop and farming activities, and the 'Croust House' restaurant, with furnishings designed and made from their own wood by Toby Roskilly, and decorated with stained glass by his sister Bryn. There had always been ponds at Tregellast, but the present upper ponds were dug out in 1978 after the droughts of 1976, and ever since have been filled naturally by springs. The lower ponds followed in 1984–7. All are stocked with carp and tench. They have since been colonized by wild mallard, moorhens, the occasional tufted duck and many other birds, as well as dragonflies, butterflies and other insects. Near the lower ponds are old withy beds, originally copsed by fishermen to make their crab-pots. There has been a continuous policy of tree-planting, with the help of the Cornwall Tree Planting Scheme, so that well over 2,000 trees are now flourishing. Around the upper ponds are many indigenous trees – oak, ash, sycamore, alder, hawthorne and many others, but interspersed among them are rarer and ornamental varieties – walnut, copper beech, two varieties of chestnut, the balsam poplar beloved of bees, cherry, and eucalyptus. Tregellast won an award from the Cornwall Farmer Wildlife Group, and was joint second in the *Country Life* Annual Conservation Award 1984. These most attractive and rewarding ponds and woodland walk are freely open under the Countryside Stewardship Scheme.

open	May–Sep, not Mon, by appointment, pm
directions	SW42 23, from Newlyn take B3315. Turn L to Boskenna Farm. Continue for 1ml down very narrow lane
owners	John & Sue Phillips
address	St Dellan, St Loy Cove, St Buryan, Penzance TR19 6DH
enquiries	T: 01736 810438 E: dellan. phillips@virgin.net
pronounced	St DELLan

WEST

SW42 23

size	0.8ha/2a
soil	Acid
altitude	30m
aspect	ESE, in an AGLV and AONB
rainfall	110cm/44in
temperature	Zone B
	Plant sales

The approach to St Dellan follows a steep, narrow lane bordered by tall trees. Suddenly the track emerges into the open to reveal spectacular views over the sea to Boscawen Point and across to the Lizard beyond. Named after the old cliffside chapel of St Dellan, long since demolished, the present house is set back from the shoreline, with gardens sweeping right down to the water's edge. The lower areas, of open meadow, lie on a raised beach, and parallel lines of hedging have been planted to preserve the vital shelterbelts as erosion takes its toll. Higher up, the plantsman's garden takes full advantage of the warm microclimate. Olearias, *Arbutus unedo*, and the rain tree, *Albizia saman*, mix with the towering spikes of echiums, alstroemerias and both blue and white agapanthus. A terraced area with sweeping views along the coast provides a vantage point, with a loggia smothered in a luxuriant growth of the Kiftsgate rose. Further along, Alexandra's seat, carefully positioned to catch the best of the evening sun, stands beside an aromatic camomile lawn, flanked by clematis and brilliant gazanias. Below, a natural spring flows into a lily pond with ornamental fish. Of particular note is the arboretum, which includes walnut, two types of sorbus, liriodendron and various olearias. There are three different varieties of metrosideros, including *Metrosideros excelsus*, the New Zealand Christmas tree, and Southern hemisphere myrtles. They have been in the arboretum for several years now, and the Phillips are eagerly awaiting their first flowering.

23 St Dellan

open	May, Jun Mon–Fri, am, pm; Jul–Oct Thu, Fri, am, pm. Castle: mid-Mar–Oct, daily excl Sat, am, pm
directions	SW51 29, 0.5ml from shore at Marazion by Causeway, or by ferry. Park on mainland
owners	NT and The Rt Hon. Lord St Levan DSC, DL
address	Estate Office, St Michael's Mount, Marazion TR17 0EF
enquiries	T: 01736 710507 F: 01736 719930 godolphin@manor-office.co.uk www.stmichaels mount.co.uk
EH	House: I

SW51 29

EH	Gardens: II
size	2ha/5a
soil	Lime-free
altitude	c.18m; Mount is c.22m
aspect	In an AONB
rainfall	89–102cm/35–40in
temperature	Zone B
	Plant sales

A residence of the St Aubyn family since John St Aubyn was appointed Captain there during the Civil Wars. The site of the earliest garden, which may date back to the time of the medieval nunnery, is on the south-east side, surrounded by 18th-century walls. It was described in 1833 by Thomas Rutger as then containing

> several sorts of fruits ... such as the peach, nectarine, plum, &c., with strawberries of the most delicious flavour; and there is a myrtle tree in it of many years' standing. Other half-tender exotics might, no doubt, be introduced here with safety.

Indeed, they have been. The rocky southern slopes have been extensively developed by the present Lord St Levan. These are the 19th-century terraces, with stone paths, steps, and irregular beds, stretching to the west from the walled garden, with a 'bower house' in a little wilderness out of view of the castle above, and some way along to the east. When Dr Borlase visited and sketched the Mount in 1769, there were plantations on the northern slopes, by which time the disused Civil War redoubts had already been planted out as gardens. There is a late-18th- or 19th-century ice-house cut in the rock higher up on the north side, and 19th- and 20th-century pigeon-holes built into the natural crevices. A grotto to the east of the summit, known as St Michael's Cave, was in use as a retreat during the 19th century, as it still is today.

24 St Michael's Mount

open	All year, strictly by appointment only
directions	SW72 43, 1.75ml from Chacewater on Redruth road, turn L to St Day. Scorrier House on R
owners	Mr & Mrs R.P. Williams
address	Scorrier House, Scorrier, Redruth TR16 5AU
enquiries	T: 01209 820264 E: rwill10442@ aol.com.
pronounced	SCORia
EH	House: II

WEST

SW72 43

size	4ha/10a
soil	Lime-free
altitude	115m
rainfall	114–127cm/45–50in
temperature	Zone C

Scorrier House was built and planted in 1798 by John Williams, grandson of John Williams of **Burncoose** (7), who was described as 'one of the most extensive and most successful managers of mines, as well as adventurers, the county ever produced'. The house once contained a unique collection of minerals, but the gardens were to become even more celebrated, since their gardener William Lobb (1809–63), who on their recommendation became a plant collector for Veitch's nursery, sent back plants and seed from his expeditions, which included *Fitzroya plicata* (1849), *Sequoiadendron giganteum*

353) – of which there was once an
enue at Scorrier – and *Thuja plicata*
353). The Pinetum in a 2.5 acre
ha) walled garden, where the col-
ction is planted, therefore forms one
the more important features of the
rden. There also survives what was
scribed in 1881 as 'one of the finest
d best managed Camellia walls in
gland', 116m (380ft) long and 6m
0ft) high.

The present house was rebuilt in
08, after a disastrous fire, and the
ounds greatly improved, retain-
g the lawned terrace with a ha-ha,
0m (328ft) long and one metre
gh, adorned by several handsome
assical urns. Among the other fea-
res at Scorrier are a fine conserva-
ry, which has been restored; a Folly
airy, and a Quartz Grotto garden,
th formal rose arches. A circular
atrefoil knot garden with a sundial
the centre, surrounded by beech
dging, was planted in 1989. There
also an herbaceous border.

open	At all times
directions	SW64 43, (1) Entrance to Country Park – Portreath road off A30, turn L at crossroad after 0.25ml, entrance 0.25ml on R; (2) Parking near East Lodge – follow Portreath road, after 1.5ml on L; (3) Parking on L of coast road – 1.5ml W of Portreath
owner	Cornwall County Council
address	Tehidy Country Park, Camborne
enquiries	T: 01209 714494 www.cornwall.gov.uk
pronounced	TIDDY
EH	House: II (private)

P

⊼

🐕

WEST
SW64 43

size	405ha/1,000 acres+
soil	Lime-free
altitude	c.85–60m
aspect	NW- and SE-sloping, in an AONB
rainfall	102–114cm/40–45in
temperature	Zone C

Although now sadly decayed, Tehidy – a Domesday manor – had been included among the ten Cornish gardens in Loudon's gazetteer of 1822. The manor had come by marriage to the Bassets in the 12th century, but the mansion – to designs by Thomas Edwards of Greenwich – was not begun until 1734, as a consequence of the family's increasing wealth from mining interests.

With the house came the laying out of the grounds, principally the work of Lord de Dunstanville (1757–1835), who against the odds succeeded in raising spruce, larch, Weymouth firs and other species in the shelter of *Pinus pinaster*, which served as nurse trees and were later removed. Although his skill was admired, the design was not without its critics. A writer in the *Journal of Horticulture* in 1878 informed his readers that 'One would like to see more clumps, more grouping, more individuality in the features of the grounds themselves ... instead of a series of long interminable stretches of wide walks'.

In the 20th century a reduced income from mining, profligacy, and fire, resulted in the estate being sold, to become a tuberculosis hospital. Several interesting features have now been lost. There had been a statue of the Antonine (Farnese) Flora, and a leopard in the celebrated artificial 'Coade stone' – the only specimens recorded in Cornwall. There were extensive kennels and a dogs' cemetery, an ice-house near the lake dug in 1781, and designs by Nesfield for a parterre. The house is now sumptuous apartments, and the surrounding garden is strictly private. 'Lady Bassett's Retreat' for meditation has been restored as 'The Gazebo'. The two pretty thatched *cottage ornée* lodges at the south and east entrances have survived intact.

26 Tehidy Country Park

open	All year, dawn to dusk; admission free, donations to RNLI (St Ives)
directions	SW51 39, leave A30 at roundabout W of Hayle on A3074 to St Ives. After Carbis Bay, entrance signs to Tregenna Castle on L-hand side
address	The Manager, Tregenna Castle Hotel, St Ives TR26 2DE
enquiries	T: 01736 795254 F: 01736 796066
pronounced	treGENna, hard 'g'
EH	House: II

WEST

SW51 39

size	29ha/72a
soil	Lime-free
altitude	90–60m
aspect	NE-sloping
rainfall	114–127cm/45–50in
temperature	Zone C
	Plant sales

The 'Castle' was built in 1774 on the heights above St Ives Bay for Samuel Stephens, an opulent merchant, by Daniel Freeman, master builder of Penryn, probably to the designs of John Wood of Bath. It evoked from the 'elegant' Richard Warner of Bath no more than faint praise – 'this stile [sic] of architecture may in general be pronounced as little less than absurd when adopted in modern mansions,' he wrote, yet he allowed that it might hold out 'the semblance of defensive strength, which in fact it does not possess.' Until recently, none have been found to praise the grounds except John Betjeman, who thought it 'a splendidly landscaped park with vistas of sea and headlands to the north and east ... which not even golf greens and tennis courts can destroy.' After 100 years, even the Stephens family tired of it, selling it to the directors of the Great Western Railway (GWR) in 1877, to become a five-star flagship hotel for their highly publicized 'Cornish Riviera' express – a name probably suggested by the Riviere dunes across the bay where, legend has it, the sands had buried the castle of King Harold. The original house has been extended beyond recognition, and, after the demise of the GWR, the hotel went into decline. Th present owners are the first to turn their attention to the garden as well as the house. Since 1996, the walled garden has been laid out to a design by Chel sea gold medallist John Moreland of Penzance, and planted luxuriantly with palms, bananas, and other exotic species, edged with neatly clipped box. Work is progressing on a new water garden.

open	By appointment + charity days
directions	SW72 43, off B3298, between Scorrier and St Day, 0.5ml W of St Day. White railings and gate, with lodge house
owner	James Williams
address	Tregullow, Scorrier, Redruth TR16 5AY
enquiries	T: 01209 820775 E: jpw.tregullow@ btopenworld.com.
pronounced	treGULLo
EH	House: II

WEST

SW72 43

size	6ha/15a
soil	Lime-free
altitude	105–85m
aspect	E-facing slope
rainfall	114–127cm/45–50in
temperature	Zone C
	Plant sales

The classical style house with a fine Victorian conservatory was built in 1826 for William (after 1866 Sir William) Williams on his marriage, but ha been altered and reduced in size. To the rear is an unusual ice-house, in the form of a tunnel. The par on the north is separated from the house by a low granite balustrade. The principal entrance lies to th south, where there is a small lodge with gate-piers on which, the story goes, a note was once found affixed, which read:

> Pray, Sir Billy, do not weep.
> We've stolen one of your fat sheep.
> For you are rich and we are poor,
> And when that's gone we'll come for more.

There are two walled gardens to the south-east, cut into the valley side, one of which is an unusual ova shape. The grounds consist principally of a wooded valley with sheltered slopes, planted with many fine trees, of which perhaps the most notable is the *Saxegotha conspicua*, Prince Albert's Yew, introduce in 1847 by William Lobb, who had been gardener i the neighbouring **Scorrier House** (25). The extensiv shrubberies, as is common in Cornwall, are mainly planted with rhododendrons and camellias, with some acers and magnolias. One of the more strik-ing features of Tregullow was the yew walks, one of which is still intact. Tregullow, like other Cornish gardens, suffered neglect during and after the Sec-ond World War, but since the 1970s there has been an active programme of restoration and replanting.

28 Tregullow

open	Apr–Sep, daily am, pm
directions	SW72 23, from Helston on A383 to Lizard, turn L on to B3293 to St Keverne. After 1.5ml entrance is on L at Garras
owner	Sir Ferrers Vyvyan
address	Estate Office, Trelowarren, Mawgan, Helston TR12 6AF
enquiries	T: 01326 221224 F: 01326 221440 E: info@trelowarren.com www.trelowarren.com
pronounced	treloWARRen
EH	House: I

WEST

SW72 23

size	c.13ha/32a; extensive grounds + woodland
soil	Lime-free
altitude	Highest point 100m (house 76m)
aspect	Sloping N–S from highest point to creek, in an AONB
rainfall	89–102cm/35–40in
temperature	Zone B
	Plant centre

A Domesday manor, the first garden at Trelowarren was recorded in 1428, when it was inherited by the Vyvyan family. The house was remodelled by the architect Thomas Edwards of Greenwich in the new Georgian fashion, when the chapel was also decorated with fine 'Strawberry Hill Gothic' plaster work. Later, the Pleasure Gardens to the south of the house were formed, and the estate separated from the unenclosed Lizard moorland by a ha-ha on the southern boundary of the woodland. Three walled gardens were enclosed: one, later known as 'Lady Vyvyan's Garden', was built immediately west of the north wing, utilizing stone salvaged from the fire at the old mansion of Nanswhyden, in the walls of which were placed glazed Gothick 'folly' windows, with a turret folly at one corner; another was intended as a botanic garden, where plants were to be arranged according to the systems of Linnaeus and Decandolle, with a central 'temple' for use as a library, although it is not known how far the project progressed. There are formal lawns around the house, with wide granite steps, leading up to the raised walk and pleasure gardens. Here there is a mount over 15.25m (50ft) in height, making it the highest point on the Lizard, which was known as 'Three Seas Point', since from it the Channel could be seen on both sides of the Lizard, as well as the Atlantic. Today, because of the growth of trees, only the latter is visible. Until her death in 1976, Trelowarren was well known from the writings of Lady C.C. (Clara) Vyvyan, a daughter of Mrs Powys Rogers (see **Burncoose** [7]).

29 Trelowarren

open	Mid-Feb–end Oct, Sun–Thur (+ Good Fri) am, pm; limited opening Dec
directions	SW44 31, 2ml NW of Penzance, 0.5ml W of Heamoor, 0.5ml off St Just road (A3071)
owner	NT
address	Trengwainton, Penzance TR20 8RZ
enquiries	T: 01736 363148 F: 01736 367762 E: trengwainton@ nationaltrust.org.uk www.nationaltrust .org.uk
pronounced	trengWAINton
EH	House, bothy, head gardener's cottage, kitchen garden walls II

WEST

SW44 31

EH	Gardens: II*
size	10ha/25a + c.40ha/ 100a woodland
soil	Lime-free over clay
altitude	120–175m
aspect	SE-sloping, in an AONB
rainfall	114–127cm/45–50in
temperature	Zone C
	Plant centre

A former residence of the Cornish Arundell family, but the landscaping is attributed to Sir Rose Price, Penzance stock, who had made a fortune in Jamai planting sugar. Under the direction of a Mr George Brown, he laid out plantations of conifers with elm oak, ash and beech; dug three pools; constructed a ice-house; formed a terrace; built lodges, and crea the nine walled gardens with ramped beds, which remain a feature today.

The estate, owing to family differences, did not pass to Price's son, and was eventually sold to Thomas Simon Bolitho, who enlarged the house and replaced Price's drive with the present carriageway. In 1925 Trengwainton passed to Lt-Col E.H.W. Bolitho, who set about developing the garden, aided by his cousins, the Williams of **Caerhays** (71) and Lanarth, and Canon Boscawen of Ludgvan. When George Johnstone of **Trewithen** (65) and Lawrence Johnstone of Hidcote, Gloucestershire, offered him a share in Frank Kingdon Ward's expedition to Assam and Burma in 1927–8, he readily accepted. His head gardener, Alfred Creek, became an expert in raising the seed sent by Ward, and in hybridizing rhododendrons, which were planted along the old drive. In the 1950s, George Hulbert planted a stream garden along the new drive with meconopsis, skunk cabbage, primulas and other bog plants, and the walled garden became a haven for the more tender plants, among them styrax, eucryphia, stewartia, and *Clianthus puniceus* – the 'Lobster Claw'.

In 1961 Sir Edward litho received the cov-d VMH from the RHS, d gave the estate to National Trust.

30 Trengwainton

open	Apr–Oct, daily, am, pm
directions	SW45 29, take Land's End turning on A30 roundabout W of Penzance, and follow brown signs
owner	Mr Timothy Charles Le Grice
address	Trereife Park, Penzance TR20 8TJ
enquiries	T: 01736 362750 F: 01736 366690 E: trereifepark@ btconnect.com www.trereifepark. co.uk
pronounced	TREEVE
EH	House: II*

WEST

SW45 29

size	Garden, in parkland 5.5ha/13.5a
soil	Lime-free
altitude	50–30m
aspect	SE-sloping
rainfall	114–127cm/45–50in
temperature	Zone C
	Plant sales

A fine house of the Nicholls family, who were the before the reign of Elizabeth I. Early in the 19th century the last male member of the family died at a young age, and his mother married the Rev Charles Valentine Le Grice, the boy's tutor, who became a minister of St Mary's Church, Penzanc Their son inherited the estate, which has since been the home of the Le Grice family. The last M Nicholls came from the Usticke family (pronound 'yewstick'). In about 1780 yews were planted, which now cover the south wall of the house, and which led her husband frequently to repeat the pun that there was '"yew" inside and outside the house'. A small park slopes away from the house to a lodge, but the estate was better know in the mid-20th century for its daffodils, grown by Charles Le Grice, who was well known in the industry.

31 Trereife Park

Blight's description in 1861 is still recognizable:

The beautifully wooded grounds of Trereife … first attract attention; the roadway is here arched with a long avenue of noble elms; near its extremity it is crossed by another avenue … a few yards up on the right is Trereife House, almost buried in foliage; a yew tree is trained over the front of the building, giving it the appearance of a living wall of leaves … The walks and peeps of woodland scenery around this place are very beautiful.

e garden has been restored and is a constant rk-in-progress. The parterre designed by Lyn Le ce and planted by Jen Hilliard has now become ll established, and is at its best in the spring.

Daily, am, pm, excl 25, 26 Dec; free admission to RHS members Nov–mid-Apr

SW64 30, signed from Crowntown on B3303, 3ml NW of Helston

Mr M. Sagin & Mr N. Helsby

Trevarno Manor, Crowntown, nr Helston TR13 0RU

T: 01326 574274
F: 01326 574282
E: enquiry@ trevarno.co.uk
www.trevarno.co.uk

treVARNo

WEST

W64 30

12ha/30a, in estate of *c.*304ha/750a

Lime-free

75–*c.*50m

NW–SE valley

102–114cm/40–45in

Zone C

Plant sales

John Betjeman believed that the poet Pope stayed here in the 18th century 'as a guest of the father of Dr Oliver the biscuit inventor', with whom he certainly corresponded. The present house was remodelled in 1839 by George Wightwick, the Cornish architect, for Christopher Wallis Popham, who built the walled garden and a conservatory, backed by a Gothic folly cottage facing the lakeside terrace. He was also probably responsible for the yew tunnel walk, 50m (165ft) long. The estate was bought in 1874 by William Bickford Smith, grandson of the inventor of the safety fuse. He was himself described by Betjeman as a 'learned artist', and it is to his initiative that we owe the principal elements of the present garden. He extended the lake, adding the neo-Gothic boathouse, and created formal lakeside terraces, ornamented with bedding schemes, rose gardens, and herbaceous borders, interspersed with gravel walks, which have now been simplified and grassed over. A rockery with its grotto, pool and stepped mount, was constructed on a spot where Wesley is reputed to have preached, and above it, along the main drive, a pinetum was planted with around 120 specimens. In recent years, the lake has been further enhanced by the construction of a cascade. Other features are the sundial on the side lawn, and an Edwardian summerhouse on a bank above the front lawn. Beyond is an 'Italian' garden, with a cast-iron fountain; the garden has been redesigned recently, though retaining the mature camellias and reintroducing the statuary. Work continues on the Walled Garden restoration project. In 2005, a woodland adventure play area was opened and a 2km estate walk was launched.

One of the most interesting gardens in this distr, Trevarno has the fascinating National Museum of Gardening – the largest collection of gardening antiques and ephemera in Britain.

32 Trevarno Estate Gardens & The National Museum of Gardening

open	Feb–Oct, Wed–Sun and bank holiday Mons, am, pm
directions	SW44 29, take Land's End turning on A30 roundabout W of Penzance; after 1ml turn R into Trewidden, just before Buryas Bridge
owner	A.R. Bolitho
address	Trewidden, Buryas Bridge, Penzance TR20 8TT
enquiries	T: 01736 366800 F: 01736 368142 E: alison.clough1@ btopenworld.com
EH	House: II

WEST

SW44 29

EH	Walled Garden walls + driveway walls: II
size	6ha/15a
soil	Lime-free
altitude	90–70m
aspect	S-sloping, in an AGLV
rainfall	114–127cm/45–50in
temperature	Zone C
	Plant sales

The drive climbs some 46m (150ft), for most of the way between old stone Cornish 'hedges'. The garden began to gain recognition in 1889 under Thomas Bedford Bolitho, whose gardener, George Maddern, after 45 years in 'one of the prettiest [gardens] in the west of England' in 1894 merited an obituary in the *Gardeners' Chronicle*. Trewidden contains perhaps the earliest tin workings in the county, in which the Fern Pit exhibits 'probably the best grouping of *Dicksonia antarctica* (Tree Ferns) in the Northern Hemisphere'. The shallower pits, known as 'The Burrows', also contain tree ferns. Near to the Pit, in a hollow, is the Rock Garden, with a small pool, perhaps most notable for the nearby collection of erythroniums. Thomas Bedford Bolitho had also gardened in Devon, at Greenway House on the Dart (later the residence of Agatha Christie), from which he brought a plant of the Chilean Nut, *Guevina avellana*, later described by the *Gardeners' Chronicle* as 'probably equal to any other in the country'. There are still specimens around the garden. The North Walk, to the rear of the house, contains some of the oldest plants, including a 'Champion tree' *Magnolia hypoleuca* planted in 1897 by Bolitho's daughter Mary, who married Charles Williams of Caerhayes (71). Trewidden was overshadowed in the mid-20th century by **Trengwainton** (30), but is still famous for its collection of over 300 varieties of camellias – from China, India and the Far East – and many magnolias, including Champion trees *Magnolia* 'Trewidden Belle', *M. sargentiana* robusta and *M. dawsoniana*.

Part of the Walled Garden is now open, and has summer interest in the form of a butterfly border, terraced lawns and unusual shrubs.

33 Trewidden Garden

open	May, Wed; Jun, Wed and Sun; Jul, Sun, pm
directions	SW43 25, take B3315 W from Newlyn, after 2.5ml Trewoofe is on R just before Lamorna turn
owner	Mrs H.M. Pigott
address	Trewoofe House, Lamorna, Penzance TR19 6PA
enquiries	T/F: 01736 810269
pronounced	TROVE

WEST
SW43 25

size	0.8ha/ 2a
soil	Lime-free (pH 6.5)
altitude	c.65m
aspect	In an AONB
rainfall	89–102cm/35–40in
temperature	Zone B
	Plant sales

Situated at the top of the Lamorna valley, Trewoofe House was built in 1913 by Ella and Charles Naper of the Lamorna School of artists, several of whom painted here between the First and Second World Wars. The present owner – Ella Naper's niece – began a new garden in 1975. The leat to the former mill pool (haunted, according to the antiquary Bottrell), crossed by a small bridge, offered an opportunity for the creation of an extensive bog garden, which is planted with a variety of primulas; many kinds of iris, astilbes and arums. Reclaimed granite has been used in the garden to create a series of rockeries, and there are many island beds containing New Zealand shrubs, and some azaleas, rhododendrons and camellias. There are also collections of euphorbias, hostas, hellebores, and iris. Hidden from view, the fruit garden has cordon and espalier trained trees. A conservatory by the house is well furnished with wall plants. This is one of the most remote gardens in the country, and as with all gardens in the extreme west of the peninsula, wind and salt are problems endemic to the site.

34 Trewoofe House

open	All year. Please phone
directions	SW44 25, from Newlyn take B3315 W. After 2.75ml take lane through trees opposite turn to Lamorna
owners	Mr & Mrs D. Waterson
address	Trewoofe Orchard, Lamorna, Penzance TR19 6BW
enquiries	T: 01736 810214 E: dickwaterson@ onetel.com
pronounced	TROVE

WEST

SW44 25

size	1.6ha/4a
soil	Mixed: alluvium, acid
altitude	35m
aspect	SE, in an AONB
rainfall	89–102cm/35–40in
temperature	Zone B
	Plant sales

Trewoofe Orchard is a secluded valley garden about a mile inland from Lamorna Cove. The land was originally part of the ancient Trewoofe Manor, and the name suggests it was once used for fruit growing. A small orchard area still survives. The house was constructed in 1912 by the philosopher Alfred Sidgewick and his novelist wife Cecily Ullman, who were involved in the lively social world of the Lamorna artists. The central feature of the garden is the presence of water. A stream with mossy granite boulders runs along the bottom of the valley, fringed by ferns, arums and bamboos. The water is channelled into calm pools separated by the noisy cascade of a waterfall. Close by lies another tranquil pond, surrounded by primulas and hostas, and fed from one of the numerous rills from the old mill leat that runs above the house. The water is not always a kindly presence, as in the worst of the winter weather it has been known to turn into a raging torrent, sweeping away stones and plants and leaving a trail of destruction. Beyond the stream lies the natural woodland area of mature trees, meandering pathways and banks of bluebells. Although something of a frost pocket, in spring the formal garden bright with camellias, bulbs and primroses, followed by hydrangeas, agapanthus and evening primrose. This secluded garden is rich in the bright colours of dragonflies, and the prevailing sounds are of the flowing water, the wind in the trees, and birdsong.

35 Trewoofe Orchard

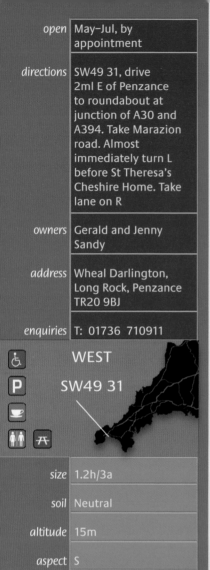

open	May–Jul, by appointment
directions	SW49 31, drive 2ml E of Penzance to roundabout at junction of A30 and A394. Take Marazion road. Almost immediately turn L before St Theresa's Cheshire Home. Take lane on R
owners	Gerald and Jenny Sandy
address	Wheal Darlington, Long Rock, Penzance TR20 9BJ
enquiries	T: 01736 710911

WEST

SW49 31

size	1.2h/3a
soil	Neutral
altitude	15m
aspect	S
rainfall	102–114cm/40–45in
temperature	Zone C

At first sight Wheal Darlington appears to focus on spacious lawns and colourful herbaceous borders, but it also contains separate, contrasting areas, half hidden by the garden buildings and shrubs. A walk along the terrace opens up a spectacular view of **St Michael's Mount** (24), framed by carefully pruned trees. This rich and varied garden has evolved gradually, and is full of plants lovingly collected over the years, each carefully labelled with full Latin description. Originally a windswept mining location, the site required much work to improve the soil, create shelterbelts, and exclude the marauding rabbits. A well-manicured leylandii hedge protects a long border, ablaze with summer flowers, and another bed of reds and purples features penstemons and lobelia. In an open position currently being developed as a prairie garden, *Stipa gigantea* already makes a dramatic impact. As a millennium tree, the Sandys planted a black mulberry descended from a specimen originally grown by James I in the Chelsea Physick Garden for his projected silk industry. Alas for him, it was the white mulberry the silkworms preferred. Wheal Darlington lies just behind the RSPB Reserve of Marazion Marsh, and numerous bird species may be spotted from the garden. Around a crystal-clear pond, primulas thrive in the bog garden. Nearby, mature trees offer welcome shade for early-flowering camellias, for rhododendrons and, in summer, for huge, strongly scented lilies. The Sandys manage to keep their plants remarkably pest-free, thanks to the ducks, which have free run of the garden.

36 Wheal Darlington

open	Last Sun Jul for NGS; May–Sep private visits and groups by appointment, pm
directions	SW47 33, from Penzance take B3311 N to Badgers Cross, turn L on road signed to Trezelah/Chysauster. After 1ml turn L to Trezelah. Entrance at bottom of lane
owners	Bryon and Barbara Cook
address	Windman Cottage, Trezelah, Gulval, Penzance TR20 8XD
enquiries	T: 01736 330688 E: barbaracook@cooptel.net

WEST
SW47 33

size	3ha/0.75a garden + 0.8ha/2a meadow
soil	Neutral to acid
altitude	25m
aspect	S, in an AONB
rainfall	101–114cm/40–45in
temperature	Zone C
	Plant sales

Windman Cottage, situated on the high ground behind Mount's Bay, defies its open location by focusing on Southern hemisphere plants, drawing inspiration from **Tresco** (1) and **St Michael's Mount** (24). In 1997, Barbara and Bryon Cook set about the task of clearing the derelict land. Granite holds the key to this garden, for it is the reuse of the plentiful stone in sheltering walls and terraces that creates its essential microclimate. Strategically placed cordyline palms and massive clumps of phormiums also help to deflect the prevailing winds. Behind the cottage, luxuriant creepers *Sollya heterophylla*, *Campsis grandiflora* and *Pandorea jasminoides* twine around the loggia. In summer, tomatoes spilling out from hanging baskets, and a heavily laden vine along the adjoining wall create a feeling of abundance. *Strelitzia reginae* flowers in the herbaceous bed below, and remains out of doors throughout the winter, as do all the plants in the garden. The range of bananas, cannas and ginger lilies, along with agapanthus and aeoniums, provides a rich, sub-tropical texture. Grass-covered mounds give landscaping on the otherwise flat site, and add valuable soil over the granite one foot below the surface. Adjacent beds display plantings of blazing orange gazanias, watsonias and eucomis, mixed with aloes and proteas. The sound of running water comes from a series of ponds with cyperus and water hyacinth, linked by a rill. Nearby, a path through the garden hedge leads to a wild meadow and a return to the outside world with wide views down to St Michael's Mount and the Lizard beyond.

37 Windman Cottage

Truro

Truro owes its origin to its position at the confluence of four rivers – the Calenick, Kenwyn, Allen and Tresillian – and to the convergence of important roads from the north, east and west. Although until recently never the county town, it has gradually increased in importance through the centuries. The wealth of the town was based upon the coinage of tin; the weekly market; an annual fair, and overseas trade. By the late 18th century, the town had grown to become the social centre of Cornwall, with its own theatre, philharmonic society, assembly rooms and, in Lemon Street, town houses modelled on those in Bath. Like that city, it began to attract many residents during the 'season', who also possessed country estates such as those at **Carclew** (121), **Tregothnan** (60), **Trelissick** (61), and the oldest of all, **Enys** (41). In the area by the Quay there are still several fine Georgian houses, built for wealthy and prominent

Truro families:
the Mansion House, Prince's House, the Great House, and the Old Mansion House, some of which once had quite elaborately designed gardens. The building of the Cathedral for the new diocese formed in 1877, and the transferring of the Law Courts from Bodmin in 1988 has finally established the city as the County Town.

(See gardens 38, 39, 41, 44, 46, 48, 5. 53, 56, 57, 60, 61, 64, 65, 67, 121.)

Falmouth

Truro was at first challenged as a port by Penryn, which received its charter as early as 1265. However, both towns were enraged when, in the 16th century the Killigrews of Arwenack had both the temerity and the foresight to realize that Smithick on their estate, nearer the sea, had the potential for an even better harbour. Falmouth now has the distinction of being the finest natural deep-sea

Truro
Falmouth
The Roseland

3 MID-WEST

rbour in Europe, although it received
charter late by Cornish standards,
1661. In its first phase it was little
ore than a fishing port, but from 1688
til the trade passed to Southampton
1852, it was the headquarters of the
yal Mail Packets, which brought with
em overseas trade and travel, making
lmouth one of the principal ports of
e county, attracting a variety of mer-
ants and speculators. Among them
re the Foxes – a west-country Quaker
mily from Wiltshire – who settled first
Bank House near Arwenack in 1759,
ening their shipping offices along the
ad, overlooking the harbour. If not the
ost important family in Falmouth, they
ilt, developed, or resided in at least 15
the properties whose gardens received
tice during the 19th century. George
oker Fox at Grove Hill became famous
submitting to the RHS of Cornwall in
37 a detailed list of 223 tender plants
at he was cultivating in the open in his

garden, for which he received a Banksian
Silver Medal. Many of these plants were
recent, but some orange and lemon trees
had been planted much earlier in the
century. Four other Fox gardens – **Fox
Rosehill** (42), **Penjerrick** (52), **Glendurgan**
(43) and **Trebah** (58) – remain among the
finest in Cornwall.

*(See gardens 40, 42, 43, 45, 47, 50, 52,
54, 62.)*

The Roseland

Today St Mawes is best known as a
yachting haven, but it too was esteemed
as a town in the 13th century, sending
two members to Parliament, and becoming a borough after the building of the
Castle in 1540. At **Lamorran House** (49),
near the Castle, since the 1980s the most
remarkable sub-tropical garden in the
county has been developing, and the
churchyard of the parish church, at **St
Just-in-Roseland** (55), is a worthy rival.

(See gardens 49, 55, 59, 63, 66.)

open	Daily, am, pm, excl 25, 26 Dec, admission free
directions	SW83 43, 0.75ml on R along turning to Malpas off Trafalgar roundabout at end of Tregolls Rd
owner	Truro City Council
location	Malpas Road, Truro
enquiries	T: 01872 274766 F: 01872 225572 E: truro@touristinfo .demon.co.uk www.truro.gov.uk
pronounced	bosCAWN

MID-WEST

SW83 43

size	Originally intended to be about 9.3ha/23a
soil	Lime-free
altitude	At river level
rainfall	102–114cm/40–45in
temperature	Zone C

The need for an area for recreation in Truro was realized as early as 1864, when an appeal was made to the Town Council. However, little was done until the late 1880s, when Lord Falmouth donated the foreshore between Waterloo Quay and the Mill Stream and the Duchy sold the adjoining foreshore between there and Sunny Corner for a nominal sum. The park was designed by F.W. Meyer, the landscape gardener at Veitch's Exeter Nurseries. In 1894 the *Gardeners Chronicle* noted that 'The plan shows extensive areas of turf devoted to sports, and breadth and openness are not lost in a too great amount of tree-planting'. The completion of the scheme depended on reclaiming land from the river, which even as late as 1934 was stated as 'still in the making, only a portion at present being complete.' This slow progress, and subsequent developments, have somewhat modified Meyer's original plan, although there are colourful ornamental bedding schemes much in the position he intended, to which has recently been added a tall sculpture created by Jonathan Craig of Penryn out of the trunk of a dying *Cupressus macrocarpa*, which as yet unnamed. The intention that the park should be used for recreation has been amply fulfilled by the provision of tennis courts, and cricket and football fields. From the foreshore there is a fine view of the Cathedral up the Truro river.

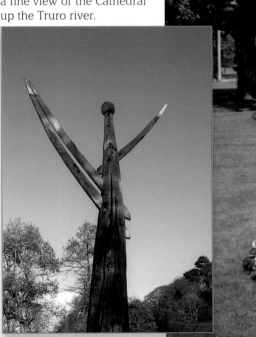

38 Boscawen Park

open	Mar–Sep, Thur, Fri, am, pm
directions	SW81 45, 0.75ml from city centre: from Higher Town, near Sainsbury's roundabout, turn down Dobbs Lane; 500yd entrance on L
owners	Michael & Wendy Perry
address	Bosvigo, Bosvigo Lane, Truro TR1 3NH
enquiries	T: 01872 275774 F: 01872 275774 E: bosvigo.plants@virgin.net www.bosvigo.com
pronounced	bosVIGo, 'I' as 'eye'
EH	House: II

MID-WEST

SW81 45

size	1ha/2a
soil	Lime-free
aspect	S
rainfall	102–114cm/40–45in
temperature	Zone C
	Nursery

There has been a house at Bosvigo since the 13th century, but the present dwelling dates from 1780 and for nearly 100 years was the residence of J.R. Paull, a Truro solicitor, and his successors. The present owners came here in 1969, at first demolishing a Victorian wing, which isolated a fine conservatory, now home to a wonderful rose, 'Marechal Ne*Pandorea jasminoides*, and many other semi-tende climbers. Their interest in gardening did not begin seriously much before 1980, since when the garde has gained increasingly widespread acclaim for its planting and association of colours. Wendy Perry been responsible for most of the planting, and her husband Michael for the landscaping and maintenance. The walled garden at the east side of the house, made possible by the demolition of the win is planted with muted colours, mostly pink and blu Beyond this is the 'Vean (Cornish 'little') Garden', in front of the Dower House, which has been quarter by pebble paths, the four beds reflecting each othe with the dominant colours gold and white with jus touch of blue. The slopes of woodland to the south the house are planted with a host of spring treasu – not the rhododendrons and camellias one might expect in a Cornish garden, but bulbs and herbaceous plants to give a jewelled effect under the big beech trees. The display starts with snowdrops, a fine collection of *Helleborus orientalis*, epimediums, erythroniums, and drifts of wood anemones. As a final surprise, tucked away in the woods is a 'Hot Garden', planted with reds, oranges and yellows, which will 'blow your socks off' in August. This is an all-season garden for the plant-lover.

39 Bosvigo

open	Daily, am, pm
directions	SW78 28, turning off Carwinion Rd S of Mawnan Smith
owners	Anthony & Jane Rogers, and NT
address	Carwinion, Mawnan Smith, Falmouth TR11 5JA
enquiries	T: 01326 250258 F: 01326 250903 E: jane@carwinion.co.uk www.carwinion.com
pronounced	carWINion

MID-WEST

SW78 28

size	3.8ha/9.5a
soil	Lime-free
altitude	65m to sea
aspect	S-facing valley, in an AONB
rainfall	102–114cm/40–45in
temperature	Zone C
	Nursery: especially bamboos

The estate was bequeathed to a younger son of the owner of **Penrose** (18), and the house was built as a residence for his son in the late 18th century. However, it was probably *his* son, Reginald Rogers (born 1854), who was responsible for the planting and design of the garden in the late 19th century, in association with the Fox family at **Glendurgan** (43) and **Trebah** (58) who were his cousins. It is possible that the family helped to finance various plant expeditions, from which they and neighbouring gardens profited. Indeed, the Carwinion valley has similarities to those at the Fox gardens, although it is longer and narrower. There are few changes from the appearance of the grounds in the early maps, although a former orchard to the south of the house has been replaced by two additional ponds, dominated by huge gunnera plants, and the walled garden has been grassed over. The present owner – a descendant of the same family – has planted camellias, eucryphias, and species rhododendrons, and in 1986 began a reference collection of some 160 species of bamboos, which are now one of the principal features, being distributed in clumps around the garden, with their names clearly labelled. Recently, the Camellia and Hydrangea Nursery formerly located at Porthtowan has transferred to Carwinion, where among its own specialities, many varieties of bamboo are available. The estate was donated to the National Trust 1969, which also owns 8ha (20 acres) of woodland. The garden remains managed by Anthony Rogers. Teas are served in summer.

40 Carwinion Bamboo Garden

Enys was the earliest garden in Cornwall to receive written mention, in a Creation play of *c.* 1450. In 1709, Camden commented on the beauty of Enys in his *Magna Britannia*. The walled garden with gazebos and walks, illustrated in Borlase's engraving of 1758, is almost certainly 17th-century. The walls are still extant though much shortened, and the pavilions have been converted into a gardener's cottage and apple store. Substantial alterations took place in the 19th century when a London architect, Henry Harrison, was engaged to work on the house and garden. He created the 'Ladies' Garden' and 'Colonel's Garden', both of which remain. They contain some of the plants surviving from the collection of J.D. Enys, who sent back many seeds and specimens from New Zealand and introduced to this country the Chatham Island Forget-me-not, *Myosotidium hortensia*. In 1907, he privately published a list of some 1,000 *Trees and Shrubs and Plants Growing at Enys*. Particular plants currently growing here are the rare Peruvian laurel, and a *Ginkgo biloba* reputed to be the tallest specimen outside Kew Gardens. There is a good collection of bamboos, including rare varieties. The lakes in the valley retain their atmosphere. Storm damage in recent

years has led to the loss of some mature trees, which has allowed the bluebells to flourish – a dramatic sight under the copper beeches in spring. Since its foundation in 2002, the Enys Trust has undertaken restoration work in the garden, and is making it increasingly available the public.

open	All year, dawn–dusk; public park, admission free
directions	Melvill Road, Falmouth
owner	Carrick District Council
enquiries	T: 01872 224307 F: 01872 272239 E: openspaces@ carrick.gov.uk www.carrick.gov.uk
EH	House: II

MID-WEST

SX08 63

size	0.8ha/2a
soil	Lime-free
altitude	From c.35m
aspect	SE-sloping
rainfall	102–114cm/40–45in
temperature	Zone C

e town house of Robert Were Fox until
 retirement in 1872, when it was sold
his nephew Howard, who was inspired
 his experience of sub-tropical plants
 his travels to design a Mediterranean-
e garden. As early as 1880, the *Gar-
ers' Chronicle* remarked that the use
cordylines 'in a novel and picturesque
nner ... form[ed] an avenue worthy of
itation'. It was, indeed, imitated along
 road into Falmouth, which was planted
d named 'Dracaena Avenue', ending just
ort of Rosehill itself. The popularity of
 Mediterranean style of planting spread
ough the seaside resorts in Cornwall
s, for example, in the **Morrab Gardens**
) in Penzance, opened in 1889 – and in
rbay in Devon, to promote tourism. In
08 Charles Curtis, editor of the *Gardeners'
agazine*, wrote about Rosehill, then having

reached its maturity – 'I cannot call to mind
one [garden] in England, that is so altogeth-
er un-English as that of Rosehill.' The whole
made up 'a picture of the character one
associates in idle moments with a "Chateau
d'Espagne"'. It was the family's intention
that Rosehill should be given to the people
of Falmouth, and to this end the greater
part of the garden was donated as a public
park, followed by the gift of the remaining
grounds and the house, which was intended to become a museum. This the local
authority felt unable to accept, and the two
became separated. The house and grounds
are now the School of Art; the remainder
– the Fox Rosehill Gardens – has interesting
exotic planting, especially the maintenance
of the former banana grove – but is now
reduced in size.

42 Fox Rosehill Gardens

open	Mid-Feb–end Oct, Tue–Sat excl Good Friday; open bank holiday Mons, am, pm
directions	SW77 27, on road to Helford passage 5ml S of Falmouth, follow NT signs
owner	NT
address	Glendurgan, Mawnan Smith, Falmouth TR11 5JZ
enquiries	T: 01872 862090 F: 01872 865808 E: glendurgan@ nationaltrust.org.uk www.nationaltrust .org.uk
pronounced	glenDERgan

MID-WEST

SW77 27

EH	Garden: II*
size	10ha/25a
soil	Lime-free over shillet with some clay
altitude	70–10m
aspect	Sloping, in an AONB
rainfall	102–114cm/40–45in
temperature	Zone C
	Plant centre

Although perhaps the best designed valley garden in Cornwall, Glendurgan escaped notice in publications until the 1930s. It was purchased by Alfred Fox – younger brother of Robert Were of **Penjerrick** (52) – in the 1820s, who planted *Pinus pinaster* as windbreaks, to which 'he added a great variety of trees and shrubs, and made several orchards'. Glendurgan is remarkable in that there have been only three head gardeners between 1825 and 1960. The valley is larger than the adjoining **Trebah** (58), but without the same direct view of the river, although running down to the picturesque fishing village of Durgan. The Maze, begun in 1833 and modelled on that at Sydney Gardens, Bath, is the best known feature of the garden, but while the foundation planting may be attributed to Alfred, little more seems to have been done until it was inherited in 1890 by his grandson, George Henry Fox, a keen botanist. It is to him that we owe many of the conifers, as well as the fragrant and tender rhododendrons. George Henry died in 1931, and was succeeded by his son Cuthbert Lloyd, who, with his wife, increased the range of species and varieties. 'Many of the plants now at their best', wrote Michael Trinick of the National Trust,

date from this period, Asiatic rhododendrons and magnolias, cornuses, camellias, hydrangeas and eucryphias ... also some unusual plants – aloe, persimmon and evergreen oleasters.

added:

Perhaps their part-
icular contribution
... was their sense of
restraint. Instead of
planting up every
corner, so tempting in
Cornwall where plants
grow quickly, they left
glades and sweeps of
grass and encouraged
wild flowers to grow
beneath the trees.

1962, on the bicentenary
the arrival of the Fox fam-
in Falmouth, Glendurgan
s donated to the National
ist.

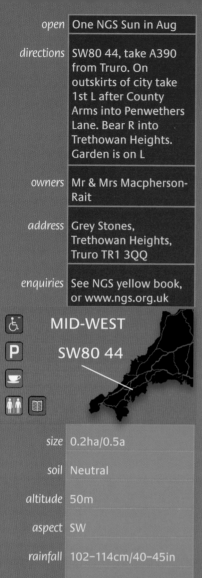

open	One NGS Sun in Aug
directions	SW80 44, take A390 from Truro. On outskirts of city take 1st L after County Arms into Penwethers Lane. Bear R into Trethowan Heights. Garden is on L
owners	Mr & Mrs Macpherson-Rait
address	Grey Stones, Trethowan Heights, Truro TR1 3QQ
enquiries	See NGS yellow book, or www.ngs.org.uk

MID-WEST
SW80 44

size	0.2ha/0.5a
soil	Neutral
altitude	50m
aspect	SW
rainfall	102–114cm/40–45in
temperature	Zone C

Colours, textures and positioning of plants are carefully controlled at Grey Stones, to provide changes of mood and tempo. At the entrance, neat leylandii hedges provide a framework for lawns, and borders recently planted in a variety of soft blues, pinks and purples. A pathway leads on through an area of light, feathery textures composed of varieties of bamboo, ornamental grasses and restios that contrast well with the surrounding gravel. Behind the house, the planting is in more exuberant style. The space has been arranged to provide interesting views from the house and raised terracing, and plants are regularly moved about to construct new perspectives. Careful siting of the sweeping flowerbeds and luxuriant foliage allow only intriguing glimpses beyond. A tropical feel is created by glowing red Bishop of Llandaff dahlias grown with clear yellow cannas, restios and aeoniums. Nearby, massive ricinus dominate, while a colour theme of blues and whites provides a cool contrast further down. A bubbling water feature of three vertical stainless steel tubes makes pleasing structural point. Hidden from the house a two ponds linked by a rill and surrounded by rodgersias, day lilies and miscanthus. Beside the house the atmosphere changes in a formal garden with a restricted colour palette of green and white design to provide an area of peace and tranquillity. Gravel pathways run between four formal beds, each with a phoenix palm and whit Japanese anemones. The entrance is flanked by a small box parterre, with cordyline palms ar bedding plants.

open	All year, am, pm; admission free
directions	SW80 31, entrances Melvill and Cliff Roads
owner	Carrick District Council
location	Melvill Road, Falmouth
enquiries	T: 01872 224307 F: 01872 272239 E: openspaces@carrick.gov.uk www.carrick.gov.uk
pronounced	gillingDOON

MID-WEST

SW80 31

size	Medium size
soil	Lime-free
aspect	S-sloping to the sea, in an AONB
rainfall	102–114cm/40–45in
temperature	Zone C

Originally 'Summerlands', Gyllyngdune was designed in 1828 by George Wightwick, a notable Cornish architect, for General William Jesser Coope, after whose death it became the residence of his son, the rector of Falmouth, who created a quite elaborate garden, with some parkland. The house is now in apartments, and the lodge, with fine iron gates, is isolated near Emslie Road. The remainder was purchased by the town in 1903 for leisure and winter gardens. The walled garden was then laid out as a lawn with bedding schemes, surrounding a central bandstand adjoining the Princess Pavilion. From this area, two sets of steps flanked by vases run down to a terrace, on which once stood stove houses for tender plants, recently demolished. From the terrace a path leads along one side of a quarry, from which the building stone for the house had been obtained, and which has been planted as a rock garden. Along this path there is a shell grotto with seats. On a prominence to the right, three slender blocks of granite form a primitive arch. There is a tunnel leading out from the floor of the quarry across Cliff Road – a later development – to a summerhouse or gazebo which, because of crosses in the gables, has been wrongly termed a 'chapel', from which steps descend to the beach. Although the greater part of this complex is designated as a leisure area, it remains an interesting relict of a once grand Victorian private garden.

Seasonal Garden Notes

Spring

- Camellias, rhododendrons & magnolias
- Frogs & toads mating, birds nesting
- New-born lambs, calves & chicks
- Daffodils, wallflowers & ranunculus
- Peach, apple, pear & quince blossom
- Rhubarb, asparagus & wild garlic

Summer

- Strawberries, peaches & raspberries
- Cornus capitata, agapanthus & verbena
- Herbs, salads, beans, spinach & potatoes
- Cornflower, cosmos, sweet pea & cleome
- Swallows, butterflies & dragonflies
- Giant rhubarb, echiums & crinodendrons

Autumn

- Bananas, kiwis, pineapples, grapes & figs
- Dahlias, chrysanthemums & nerines
- Cucurbits, onions, chillies & chard
- Berries, nuts, fungi & autumn colour
- Redwings, linnets & bramblings

Winter

- Hellebores, cyclamen & anemones
- Proteas, acacia & hardenbergia
- Leeks, roots & brassicas
- Kingfishers, bats, owls & woodpeckers
- Spreading seaweed & double digging

Over 200 varieties of mostly heritage fruit, vegetable, salad and herb are lovingly tended to supply the Heligan Tearoom with fresh, seasonal produce throughout the year.

Today the Vegetable Garden, walled Flower Garden and Melon Yard offer an enticing stage for a glorious array of traditional crops and growing methods. Learn about exotic glasshouse fruits, Victorian crop rotation and the inspiring horticultural landscape.

45 Gyllyngdune Gardens & Princess Pavilion

open	Occasionally throughout the year, strictly by appointment only
directions	SW74 37, from Falmouth take A393. Turn L at Ponsanooth Post Office. After 0.3ml turn L into drive
address	Kennall House, Ponsanooth TR3 7HJ
enquiries	T: 01872 870557
pronounced	KENNal
EH	House: II

MID-WEST
SW74 37

EH	Garden: Part of scheduled ancient monument
size	2.4ha/6a in 9.3ha/23a grounds
soil	Acid
altitude	55m
aspect	Valley garden
rainfall	127–152cm/50–60in
temperature	Zone C

This is a distinctive valley garden, where the Kenn River flows between steep wooded banks. It was t location of the Kennal Vale Gunpowder Works, a k component in the Cornish mining industry as sup er of most of the explosives used in the county. Th elegant house was formerly occupied by the mana er. The grounds contain a mixture of typically Brit species, and the exotics that will grow in Cornwall favourable conditions. The owners have taken on regeneration of the previous garden features and the improvement of the wider grounds. A Victoria walled garden reached by a wooden bridge has been richly planted with a wide variety of trees, shrubs and herbaceous plants. The high walls provide an especially sheltered environment for rodgersia, cornus, acer, tree ferns and bananas. Rich colouring is supplied in late summer by the vibrant shades of *Cercidiphyllum japonicum*. The weeping branches of *Cupressus cashmeriana* give particular distinction to one corner. Outside the walled garden are numerous bamboo varieties, and huge *Rhododendron arboreum*. The garden has a series of ponds, fed from the Kennal River. In one, a reconstructed island has been planted with the feathery fronds of pampas grass and acers. Above the house, terraces have been created by levelling out the ground, and the massive blocks of granite have been used elsewhere in the grounds to add structure to the planting. The surrounding woods are laced with pathways, and in early summer are a sea of bluebells and dainty white wood anemones.

46 Kennall House

open	Daily am, pm, admission free
owner	Falmouth Town Council
location	Kimberley Park Road, Falmouth
enquiries	T: 01326 315559 F: 01326 312662 E: mark@falmouth towncouncil.com www.falmouthtown council.com

MID-WEST

SX08 63

size	c.2.8ha/7a
soil	Lime-free
altitude	30m
aspect	E-sloping
rainfall	102–114cm/40–45in
temperature	Zone C

The land for this park was presented to the town in 1877 by the Earl of Kimberley, as an ornamental recreation ground, which was then laid out by John Simpson Tyerman, formerly of the Liverpool Botanic Gardens, who lived at Penlee House in Tregony. The opening was announced in *The Times* of 26 May, and was considered notable enough for Edgar Thurston to include it among the select gardens in his *Trees and Shrubs of Cornwall* (1930), where he cited 15 trees. The Dracaenas (*Cordylines*) also received a mention in the *Garden* of 1880, and the *Gardeners' Chronicle* referred to plants submitted to the Falmouth Naturalists' Association exhibition in 1889. In recent years, a banana plant at the lower

rance has been a notable
ture. From the road, the
lding schemes are most
minent, but the other side
the valley is more wooded,
l has a pond. The Earl of
nberley (in Norfolk) had
erited the ancient estates
the Killigrews of Arwenack
Falmouth, by way of the
keley family, hence the
-Cornish names of both
Park and the Vale.

47 Kimberley Park

open	One Sun each Apr and May, pm, or by appointment
directions	SW89 50, off B3275, by Ladock Church
owner	Mr G.J. Holborow
address	Ladock House, Ladock, Truro TR2 4PL
enquiries	T: 01726 882274 F: 01726 883580
pronounced	LADock
EH	House: II

MID-WEST

SW89 50

size	1.6ha/4a
soil	Lime-free
altitude	50m
rainfall	102–114cm/40–45in
temperature	Zone D
	Plant sales

Built in 1820 as the rectory for the parish of Ladock, the house is well sited on a platform looking west over the valley and south over a wide lawn. Many fine trees have survived from these early times, standing proud with strong trunks, having resisted the heavy gales that afflicted Cornwall in the 1980s and 1990s. When the present owners came into residence in 1968, the house was somewhat dilapidated, and the grounds overgrown. Undergrowth was cleared, and trees thinned out, so that what was once dense woodland has become an area with widely spaced mature trees forming a high canopy above wide grass walks, sheltered by well-placed banks of the original laurel or aucuba. This plan has provided a splendid opportunity for the planting of rhododendrons, azaleas and camellias, which now form the principal attraction of this garden in springtime, when the ground is carpeted with bluebells. Many Cornish gardens grow these plants, but here they have been carefully selected, or have been received from notable sources such as **Trewithen** (65) and **Lamellen** (125).

To the west of the house is a meadow, in the middle of which grows a magnificent, wide-spreading, Turkey oak. A new garden is being developed on the far side of this field, seen from the house, and accessed around the side. Here and there new and striking trees have been planted, among which the birch *Betula jacquemontii*, with its white bark, stands out. A bank of hydrangeas of various tints provides a splash of colour along the side of the lawn in summer.

48 Ladock House

open	Apr–Sep, Wed, Fri, am, pm
directions	SW84 33, 1st turning R after garage; signposted to St Mawes Castle, entrance 0.5ml on L
owners	R. & M. Dudley-Cooke
address	Lamorran House, Upper Castle Road, St Mawes TR2 5BZ
enquiries	T: 01326 270800 F: 01326 270801
pronounced	LaMORan

MID-WEST

SW84 33

size	1.8ha/4.5a
soil	Lime-free
altitude	60–15m
aspect	SE-sloping, in an AONB
rainfall	89–102cm/35–40in
temperature	Zone C

The garden at Lamorran House was re-created by Robert Dudley-Cooke, who moved from his house in Surrey in 1982, bringing with him many rhododendrons, and particularly evergreen azaleas, of which there are 500 specimens, some of which had begun their life in Cornwall. The Japanese Garden with a waterfall and grotto was the first to be formed, and this was followed by work on the lower garden, which at that time was overgrown with blackthorn and brambles. Here a Mediterranean-type garden was created, surmounted by a small temple, and an Italianate pond. It has been necessary to provide shelter from the south-west wind from Falmouth, and scorching easterlies in the early year. Where protected, such plants as acacias, of which there are 33 species, callistemons, grevilleas, cassias, metrosideros and *Albizia lophantha* are flourishing. On the succulent banks there is a selection of agaves and lampranthus, with bougainvillaea growing in the walled garden and beneath the temple. Travels in the Mediterranean region inspired an enthusiasm for palms, of which there are over 200 in the garden, representing over 35 different species, including mature *Phoenix* and *Butia* varieties. There are a growing number of tree ferns, with the emphasis on the tender *Cyathea* species, particularly the black-stemmed *Medularis*. The various forms of yucca, dasylirion, beschorneria, and the succulents such as aeoniums and echeverias all add to the sub-tropical effect. This fascinating and unique garden continues an earlier tradition in the acclimatization of exotics, most notably at the Fox family gardens in Falmouth at Grove Hill, and **Fox Rosehill** (42).

49 Lamorran House Gardens

open	Daily, am to dusk; entrance: donation to charity
directions	SW81 37, N out of Mylor to Restonguet Passage; take road signed to Pandora Inn, entrance on R
owners	Mrs H. Hall
address	Lanterns, Restronguet Hill, Mylor, Falmouth TR11 5ST
enquiries	T: 01326 372007

MID-WEST

SW81 37

size	0.2ha/0.5a
soil	Lime-free
altitude	Near river level
aspect	In an AONB
rainfall	102–114cm/40–45in
temperature	Zone C
	Plant sales

Lanterns, through which a stream runs to Restronguet Creek, lies above the Pandora Inn. This is a plantsman's garden, begun in 1966, with a wide-ranging collection of species and varieties, both for the waterside and dry areas. By reason of its position it is possible to grow tender plants such as *Parochetus communis*, and the *Salvias elegans* 'Scarlett Pineapple' and *guarantica* in the open all year round. Alpines, always unreliable in the damp Cornish climate, are rarely attempted, but here *Soldanella villosa*, which is notoriously difficult to flower, flourishes. More intensive cultivation is made possible by the use of the two heated greenhouses, and a conservatory.

50 Lanterns

open	One Sun each, Apr, May, pm; groups by appointment
directions	SW89 50, on R entering Ladock from Tresillian on B3275. Park in Falmouth Arms or parish hall, with permission
owners	Mr & Mrs Michael Cole
address	Nansawsan House, Ladock, Truro TR2 4PW
enquiries	T: 01726 882392
pronounced	nanSAWsan

SW89 50

MID-WEST

size	0.6ha/1.5a
soil	Lime-free
altitude	35m
rainfall	102–114cm/40–45in
temperature	Zone D
	Plant sales

Originally the curate's house at Ladock, occupied by the Revd Stamford Raffles Flint, the great-nephew of Sir Thomas Stamford Raffles, who established the settlement at Singapore, and grandson of Maj.-Gen. William Mudge, who carried out the first Ordnance Survey of Britain. As he became elevated from curate to rector, to a Canon, and finally to Archdeacon, so he enlarged his house and grounds. His daughter Alison married George Johnstone of **Trewithen** (65), who became his executor. The present house consists of the main entrance and west wing, with a substantial part of the original garden. From the terrace there is a view over a wide lawn to the countryside beyond. A small conservatory houses tender plants, including two lapagerias – one rose, the other white. There is a mixed border below the terrace, and the perimeter of the lawn is well furnished with shrubs and trees, with a *Cercis siliquastrum*, the Judas Tree, near the terrace.

The principal interest and attraction lies in the secret gardens in the shrubberies to the west of the lawn. At the far end, trellis work surrounds a small pond, from which paths thread through plantations of rhododendrons and camellias, for this is essentially a spring garden. Beyond is a narrow lawn with a summerhouse at one end and a greenhouse at the other, in which a plumbago and ipomoea are growing. What distinguishes this garden is the number of identified old Cornish hybrids, bred by Samuel Smith at **Penjerrick** (52), and the Gills at **Tremough** (62, and page 10). Michael Cole is also pursuing his interest in the beautiful, but now neglected Ghent azaleas. A visit to this garden will repay those interested in these classic plants, while the mass of colour will attract the non-specialist.

51 Nansawsan House

open	Mar–Sep, Wed–Fri, Sun, pm, or by appointment
directions	SW77 30, 3ml SW of Falmouth between Budock and Mawnan Smith, opposite Penmorvah Manor Hotel
owner	Mrs Rachel Morin
address	Odd Acre, Penpol, Devoran, Truro TR3 6NW
enquiries	T: 01872 870105
pronounced	penJERRick

P MID-WEST

SW77 30

EH	Gardens: II
size	4ha/10a
soil	Lime-free
altitude	80–10m
aspect	SE-sloping, in an AONB
rainfall	102–114cm/40–45in
temperature	Zone C

The earliest and archetypal Cornish valley garden – a genre often dismissed as without conscious (or evident) design. Early records show this to be far from true. Robert Were Fox of **Rosehill** (42) farmed there for several years, and the estate came into his possession in 1839, when he handed over its management to his son Barclay, who began to lay out the grounds, digging pools, planting, and extending the house to become a family retreat. Barclay died in 1855, his father outliving him by 22 years. He had already begun experiments with exotic plants at Rosehill, and took this enthusiasm to Penjerrick on his retirement in 1872. A writer in the *Gardeners' Chronicle* of 1874 emphasized that the beauty of Penjerrick at that time depended on more than nature:

> The spot is naturally lovely, but not exceptionally so ... but I doubt if there is [anywhere] which can compete with Penjerrick in a certain indescribable effect – the effect of landscape gardening carried out with the most exquisitely cultivated taste.

After R.W. Fox's death in 1877, his only surviving daughter, Anna Maria, continued to reside there an develop the garden until her death in 1897. The he gardener, Samuel Smith, who had been appointed in 1889, was responsible for most of the plantings of rhododendrons, and proved an expert hybridize. The old house – 'too small to be designated a mansion and far too romantic to be called a villa' – was replaced by the present dwelling in 1935. In 1987 Penjerrick was left by Janet Fox to the National Tru who turned it down. The present owner prefers the garden jungle-like, so gumboots are recommended footwear. Penjerrick was featured on Channel Four in 2001.

52 Penjerrick Garden

open	All year round for charity, by appointment
directions	SW82 38, A39 from Truro, turn on to B3289 at Playing Place to first crossroads, straight on 0.5ml short of Feock village
owner	Mrs Hilda Davey
address	Polgwynne, Feock, Truro TR3 6SG
enquiries	T: 01872 862612
pronounced	polGWIN

MID-WEST

SW82 38

size	1.8ha/4.5a
soil	Lime-free
altitude	30m–sea
aspect	SE-sloping, in an AONB
rainfall	102–114cm/40–45in
temperature	Zone C

Built to the east of Porthgwidden in one of the walled gardens in 1935, by Mr and Mrs H.K. Neale, who lived there from 1936 to 1947. At that time it occupied about six acres (2.4ha). The present grounds, developed since 1966, are smaller, but they include part of the plantation from Porthgwidden down to the sea, which was added as a protection against further development. The garden falls away in three terraces. The first, of stone, is in front of the house, from which there are views across the lawns to the estuary beyond. The second terrace is a large rectangular lawn. On the west is a bed of shrubs, beyond which, through a doorway, is entered a small, formal walled garden with a rectangular pond. Beyond this is a much larger walled garden, now grassed over, in which are the greenhouses whose mechanisms were described by Canon Phillpotts in the *Journal* of the RHS in 1852. Across the lawn of the third terrace a rill runs into the foliage below, where, in the south-east corner there is a summerhouse. The whole garden is beautifully designed and richly planted. It includes what is believed to be the largest female *Ginkgo biloba* in Britain.

53 Polgwynne

open	Daily, am, pm, admission free
directions	SW80 31, W end of Cliff Road
owners	Carrick District Council
address	Gyllyngvase Beach, Seafront, Cliff Road, Falmouth
enquiries	T: 01872 224307 F: 01872 272239 E: openspaces @carrick.gov.uk www.carrick.gov.uk

SW80 31
MID-WEST

size	Small
soil	Neutral
altitude	Shore level
aspect	In an AONB
rainfall	102–114cm/40–45in
temperature	Zone C

Named after the wife of George V, the 'Queen Mary Gardens, opposite the bathing beach,' so a *Directory* states, 'were opened to the public in 1913, and were the gift of the Earl of Kimberley, the cost of laying them out being borne by the Hon. Mrs. C.S. Goldman [wife of the MP]; in front is a new promenade.' The Earl had already (in 1877) presented the town with the **Kimberley Park** (47), which was named after him. In 1903 the Council had purchased the **Gyllyngdune** estate (45), which until then occupied the land right down to the beach. This provided the opportunity to extend the road, thus creating a promenade the whole length of the cliff, up to and beyond the Falmouth Hotel. The laying out of the Queen Mary Gardens formed a part of the development of Gyllyngvase into the principal 'bathing' beach of the resort. Since then the Gardens have regularly been the scene of colourful bedding schemes, and the planting of exotics, such as agaves, aloes and puyas.

54 Queen Mary Gardens

open	Daily
directions	SW84 35, turning off A3078 2ml before St Mawes
address	The Vicar, 16 Waterloo Close, St Mawes, Truro TR2 5BD
enquiries	T: 01326 270248

MID-WEST

SW84 35

size	Medium-sized churchyard + memorial garden
soil	Lime-free
altitude	30m to sea
aspect	Steeply N-sloping, in an AONB
rainfall	89–102cm/35–40in
temperature	Zone C

Described by Gilbert in his *Historical Survey* (1822) as being in a 'sequestered nook', and 'a valuable subject for the pencil of the artist, and admirers of landscape scenery.' In 1859 Murray's *Guide* advised that it was 'worth visiting', and many thousands have done so ever since. It seems probable that Edward Rodd, who was rector from 1803 to 1836, brought with him the horticultural expertise of his family at **Trebartha** (117) in North Hill – which he inherited in 1836 – and originated the plantings in the churchyard, which were considerably enhanced later in the century, when John Garland Treseder returned from Australia and founded a nursery alongside. Among the embellishments were a series of granite stones inscribed with verses and epigrams, lining the path down to the church, placed there by the Revd Humphrey Davis, rector from 1901 to 1930. In 1984 the Manpower Services Commission set up a project to enlarge the churchyard to designs by Neil, the grandson of J.G. Treseder, to include a pool fed by a rill. As a result of a legacy from Mrs Anne Groves, it became possible at the same time to lay out the opposite side of the road to the churchyard as Memorial Gardens, which have opened up new and higher vistas to the Creek.

55 St Just-in-Roseland Churchyard

<table>
<tr><td>open</td><td>Various in May, Jun, Jul, pm, or by appointment</td></tr>
<tr><td>directions</td><td>SW79 48, turn off B3284 by Nature Reserve at Allet; farm is on R</td></tr>
<tr><td>owner</td><td>Mrs J.M. Cook</td></tr>
<tr><td>address</td><td>Springfield Farm, Allet, Truro TR4 9DJ</td></tr>
<tr><td>enquiries</td><td>T: 01872 540492</td></tr>
</table>

MID-WEST

SW79 48

<table>
<tr><td>size</td><td>1ha/2.5a</td></tr>
<tr><td>soil</td><td>Neutral to acid</td></tr>
<tr><td>altitude</td><td>85m</td></tr>
<tr><td>aspect</td><td>SE</td></tr>
<tr><td>rainfall</td><td>89–102cm/35–40in</td></tr>
<tr><td>temperature</td><td>Zone D</td></tr>
<tr><td></td><td>Plant sales</td></tr>
</table>

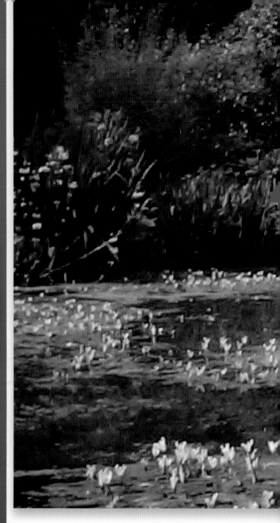

The garden at Springfield Farm arose entirely as a result of the owner's enthusiasm for horticulture, which led to her planting up this former meadow chiefly for her own interest. It is therefore of an informal design, laid out in sweeping island beds suited to contain the chosen shrubs and herbaceous specimens selected by a plantswoman. Towards the low end of the garden, on the right, a marshy area with a natural pond, now crossed by a bridge, presented an opportunity for the creation of a bog and water garden. The pond contains mainly water lilies and aponogetum, and has been edged with herbaceous plants and shrubs. Nearby is an area of woodland where magnolias, camellias and rhododendrons have been introduced, underplanted with daffodils and erythroniums. This garden was begun in 198 and is now reaching its maturity.

56 Springfield Farm

open	Mid-Jun–mid-Jul, Sat, Sun, pm, by appointment
directions	SW80 53, 1ml off A30 on B3285 towards Goonhavern and Perranporth
owners	Diana & Michael Craig
address	Talisonny House, Goonhavern, Truro TR4 9QG
enquiries	T: 01872 540336 F: 01872 540460
pronounced	TALisony

MID-WEST

SW80 53

size	4ha/10a
soil	Neutral to acid
altitude	92m
aspect	SW
rainfall	89–102cm/35–40in
temperature	Zone D
	Plant sales

The garden, which is in the south-west corner of a large field, was begun in 1994, following the Craigs' move from the Isle of Wight in 1972. The house, which is towards the west side of the garden, faces south, with a sun-room projecting on to a terrace lined with pot plants, one containing a splendid display of isoplexis. Among the climbers on the wall are roses, a *Clematis armandii*, jasmine, two forms of passion flower, and the climbing *Hydrangea seemannii*. Running out in line with the sun-room is a substantial pergola, with climbing roses and clematis, including the beautiful *C. florida* 'Sieboldii'; a wisteria; a fremontodendron, and other plants needing support. The boundaries of the garden are planted with conifers of various hues, backed by hedging trees, in front of which are a pineapple guava, *Acca sellowiana*, and other interesting trees and shrubs spaced as lawn specimens. Around the sides of the garden are large herbaceous borders, two of which, to the right of the pergola, form two facing arcs of a circle, the one planted with alstroemeria, the other with dahlias. To the rear of the house, the area is divided in two by a trellis with roses; the smaller part, to the east, is planted with specimen trees and bedding; to the west is partly fruit orchard, with the remainder devoted to vegetables. Along this west boundary, a stream extends the whole length of the field, down which is a long chain of semi-c cular mixed shrub and herbaceous beds, each wit various plantings – one, for instance, with cordylir phormiums and other exotic plants. The field itsel mown and planted with several specimen trees ar clumps. This garden has a vast range of plants to interest the plantsman, in a most attractive setting

57 Talisonny House

open	Daily all year, am, pm; entry free to RHS members
directions	SW76 27, follow brown signs from roundabout at junction of A39 and A394 NW of Falmouth
owner	Trebah Garden Trust
address	Trebah, Mawnan Smith, Falmouth TR11 5JZ
enquiries	T: 01326 250448 F: 01326 250781 E: mail@ trebah-garden.co.uk www.trebah-garden .co.uk
pronounced	TREBBA, usually anglicized to TREEbaa

MID-WEST

SW76 27

EH	Gardens: II
size	10.5ha/26a
soil	Lime-free
altitude	65m to estuary
aspect	S-sloping valley, in an AONB
rainfall	102–114cm/40–45in
temperature	Zone C
	Plant centre

The present house was built for the Nicholls family in about 1750, and was later acquired by Charles Fox, youngest brother of the **Penjerrick** (52) and **Glendurgan** (43) Foxes. Within a shelterbelt of *Pinus pinaster* and *P. radiata*, around the rim of the 26-acre valley running down to the Helford River, Charles Fox planted an arboretum as a pleasure garden. The estate was inherited by Fox's daughter Juliet and her husband Edmund Backhouse, MP, and after Charles Fox's death in 1876, the Backhouse family introduced the exotic collections of Mediterranean and sub-tropical flora for which Trebah has become famous. The garden was further developed by Charles and Alice Hext, who bought Trebah in 1907, and created the present Mallard Pond, which became home to a flock of pink flamingoes. By the mid-20th century, Bishop Hunkin was of the opinion that it was under the Hexts that the garden 'certainly reached its height'. As in the other Fox gardens, the hybridizing of rhododendrons flourished, producing the lovely 'Trebah Glory' and 'Trebah Gem'. After the death of Alice Hext in 1939, the estate was sold off in small parcels, and for the next 42 years the house and garden fell into decay. Trebah was bought by the Hibbert family in 1981, and they began a long programme of restoration and development. They opened the garden to the public in 1987, and three years later created the Trebah Garden Trust, donating to it the house, garden and cottages. In recent years, Trebah has received grants from the Heritage Lottery Fund and Objective One for a new visitor centre and garden enhancement. It is now one of the leading attractions in Cornwall, and the garden has been secured for the enjoyment of the public for all time.

open	One Sun in Apr, pm, and during village festival in Jun
directions	SW91 39, adjoining Trist House
owners	Dr & Mrs A.G. Cowen
address	Tregarthen, Veryan, Truro TR2 5QA
enquiries	T: 01872 501542
pronounced	treGARTHen

MID-WEST

SW91 39

size	c.0.4ha/1a
soil	Lime-free
altitude	75m
aspect	In an AONB
rainfall	89–102cm/35–40in
temperature	Zone C

A contemporary bungalow, Tregarthen is reached at the top of the drive alongside the Village Stores/Post Office. It can also be entered from **Trist House** (66) when it is opened at the same time. The path runs from the remarkable rockery, entering the wild part of Tregarthen through a gate and thence, via a bridge over the stream with many water plants, to the main lawn, and a terrace at the rear of the house, overhung with wisteria. The main garden rises up steps from the lawn, which is planted in mixed shrub and flower borders overtopped with trees. From this area, above the side of the house, runs a long pergola covered with roses and wisteria, which opens into three compartments, one with vegetables, another with a sundial. The path then sweeps down to the front of the house, where, among other trees are mature magnolias, including the fine *Magnolia* 'Star Wars'. The garden has been developing since 1994, and was opened for the first time in 2000.

59 Tregarthen

open	One weekend, Mar or Apr. All year by appointment for individuals or groups
directions	SW85 41, from Truro E on A30. At Tresillian Bridge turn R to St Michael Penkivel. After 3.5ml turn L to Tregothnan Estate. Sign to Estate Office
owners	The Hon. E.A.H. Boscawen
address	Tregothnan, St Michael Penkivel, Truro TR2 4AN
enquiries	T: 01872 520022 F: 01872 520291 E: garden@ tregothnan.com www.tregothnan.com
pronounced	treGOTHnan
EH	House: I

MID-WEST

SW85 41

EH	Gardens: II* and II
size	40.5ha/100a
soil	Acid
altitude	70m
aspect	SW, in an AONB
rainfall	110cm/45in
temperature	Zone C
	Nursery

Tregothnan is an intriguing mixture of the traditional and the new. The Boscawen family, in occupation since the 14th century, commissioned the celebrated landscape designer Humphry Repton to draw up plans for both house and garden. The house was subsequently remodelled, opening up the dramatic vista from the house to the River Fal. Extensive planting was carried out in the 19th century by Evelyn, 6th Viscount, and his brother, the notable horticulturist the Revd John Townsend Boscawen, Rector of Lamorran. Evidence of the early planting is revealed in the displays of mature rhododendrons and camellias. Garden walks are delineated by avenues of lime, trachycarpus or myrtle, and in early summer sheets of bluebells cover the ground beneath mature trees. The old bowling green survives, and Tregothnan also retains one of the few deer parks in Cornwall (see page 8). The present occupant, the Honourable Evelyn Boscawen, is continuing the horticultural tradition. The arboretum contains a considerable range of species, and unusual plants are continually added to the grounds. A new water parterre, overlooked by Admiral Boscawen's cannons, has been created below the terrace of the house. A summerhouse styled as a Nepalese teahouse overlooks the Himalayan Valley and work is in hand on the South American garden, partly stocked with plants from the expeditions of the current Head Gardener, Jonathon Jones. A newly planted camellia maze is growing well.

A major enterprise is the creation of a tea plantation aimed at producing high quality products for the exclusive London markets.

140

Daily, mid-Feb–23 Dec, am, pm; 27 Dec–mid-Feb, Thu–Sun, am, pm	
SW83 39, off A39 Truro–Falmouth road at Playing Place, on B3289 to King Harry Ferry; just before ferry	
NT	
Trelissick, Feock, Truro TR3 6QL	
T: 01872 862090 F: 01872 865808 E: trelissick@national trust.org.uk www. nationaltrust.org.uk	
treLISsick	
House: II*; water-tower, etc, II	

ID-WEST
W83 39

Gardens: II*	
8ha/20a + 152ha/376a parkland	
Shillet on clay, lime-free	
50m to river	
E-sloping, in an AONB	
102–114cm/40–45in	
Zone C	
Photinias and Azaras	
Plant centre	

Descriptions of Trelissick have focused on the parkland, which is of a kind unusual in Cornwall. The first modern house was built in about 1750 to designs by Edmund Davy, grandfather of the celebrated Humphry Davy. The estate was bought in 1790 by the wealthy mine-owner 'guinea-a-minute' Daniell, whose son, Thomas, engaged Peter Frederick Robinson in 1824 to rebuild the house, described by Pevsner as 'the sever-est neo-Greek mansion in Cornwall'. He laid out exten-sive rides through the beauti-ful hanging woods along the west side of the estuary, and planted particularly beech and deciduous oaks in the park. However, his extravagant style of life eventually obliged him to sell his estate. By 1854 it had passed to Carew Davies Gilbert, who raised a sec-ond storey on the wings of the house; introduced 'a fair sprinkling of foreign trees and shrubs from his wander-ings into remote regions of the globe', and began laying out the Carcaddon area, over the bridge, as a garden. In the 1930s the estate was still largely shrubberies beneath a canopy of oak and beech, with some fine conifers.

The present garden is the creation of Mrs Ida Copeland and her husband Ronald, a director of Spode – many of the flowers painted on their porcelain being grown at Trelissick. Together they planted the garden and the Dell with trees and shrubs, including hybrid rhododendrons from Bodnant, from 1928 onwards. In 1955 Mrs Copeland donated the property to the National Trust, who opened up the vista to **Tregothnan** (60). Among the many features, the log summerhouse, and the water-tower with its squirrel weather-vane, from the crest of the Gilbert family, are noteworthy.

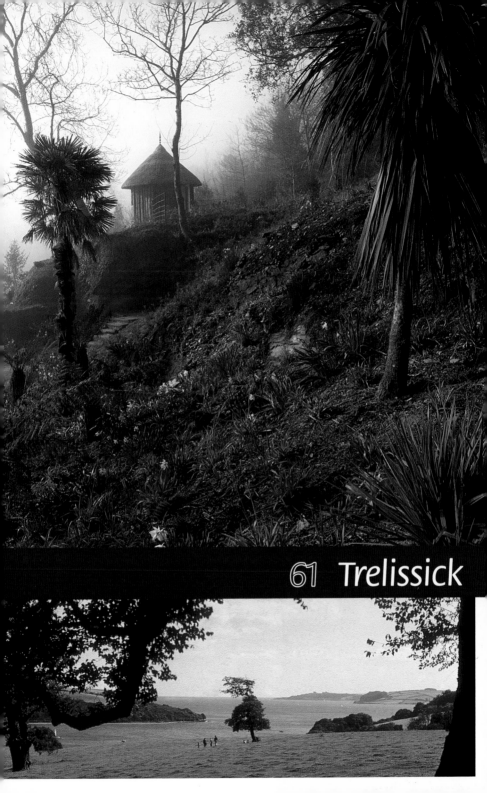

open	All year, by appointment only
directions	SW76 34, from Falmouth take Penryn bypass towards Truro. At Treliever roundabout turn R, signed CUC Tremough Campus. Entrance 100yd on R. Some campus facilities, normal opening times
owner	University College Falmouth
address	Tremough Campus, Penryn TR10 9EZ
enquiries	T: 01326 370400
pronounced	treMOH
EH	House: II

MID-WEST

SW76 34

EH	Gardens: Parts II
size	4ha/10a in 29ha/72a campus
soil	Acid
altitude	100m
aspect	SE
rainfall	102cm/40in
temperature	Zone C

Tremough is now a university campus, developed as part of the Combined Universities in Cornwall. The historic side of the property was created in the early 18th century by John Worth, successful Penryn landowner and businessman who became Sheriff of Cornwall. He built the mansion house and planted the lime avenue to create a dramatic framework for the façade. In the 19th century, much work was carried out by Benjamin Sampson, who constructed an Italian garden, overlooked by terraces planted with specimen magnolias and azaleas. He converted the walled kitchen garden into an exotic pleasure garden, and set about restoring the grounds, for which he bought specimens from the famous Veitch Nursery. Subsequent owners were the Shilson family, already keen horticulturists. They received seed from the Sikkim expedition of Joseph Hooker, and Tremough became notable for its numerous *Rhododendron arboreum*. Head Gardener Richard Gill (see page 10) became an expert hybridizer of rhododendrons, and produced numerous varieties that were widely exported. His most famous hybrid, Beauty of Tremough, still flourishes in the garden. Many rhododendron specimens survive in the grounds, producing dramatic displays of flower in early summer. The walled garden contains the remains of the original Paxton greenhouses, and is also the location of a productive orchard that includes local varieties. The ornamental pond is now dominated by massive magnolias, and the ground is thick with primroses in season. The estate also contains a grotto, and a memorial to the American forces of the Second World War, stationed in Cornwall in preparation for the D-Day landings.

62 Tremough

open	One Sun May, Aug, pm, and by appointment
directions	SW75 28, on Truro to Helston/Falmouth road, A39/A394. Follow signs for Constantine, at High Cross garage, 1.5ml before Constantine, turn L signed Mawnan, R after 30yd down dead-end lane: 0.5ml at end of lane
owner	Mrs Lucie Nottingham
address	Trenarth, Constantine TR11 5JN
enquiries	T/F: 01326 340444 E: lmnottingham@ tiscali.net
pronounced	treNARTH
EH	House: II

MID-WEST

SW75 28

EH	Gardens: 18th-C garden walls II
size	0.8ha/3a
soil	Lime-free
altitude	From 50m
aspect	SE-sloping, in an AONB
rainfall	102–114cm/40–45in
temperature	Zone C

The grounds are entered by way of a wide approach that opens on to a view of the countryside beyond, where the woods run down the valley to the Helford river. A right turn on the drive reveals the Georgian-fronted farmhouse below, where the mildness of the climate is at once evidenced by the sight of a large, 9ft high *Daphne bholua*, and a variety of cannas and hedychiums. The main ornamental gardens are on the terraced slopes above the house, enclosed on three sides by a long garden wall, listed by English Heritage. Within these walls, clad with tender climbers, are yew 'rooms' containing rockery and herbaceous beds, a pergola, a vegetable garden, and a newly restored potting shed. The main drive is planted with camellias and hellebores for early spring colour; crocosmias and kniphofias in hot summer beds, and hydrangeas and Japanese anemones for cooler late summer and autumn interest.

To the rear of the house, an arch leads into an attractive Elizabethan courtyard, which has the date 1658, and the arms of Trenarth and Trefusis with the motto 'GOD GIVETH STRENGTH' on a lead plaque over the doorway.

Below the house further terraces drop dow areas of less formal planting, which include a holm oak walk, a puddled-clay pond, small b garden, and large orchard with chickens. Tre exhibits a charming association of modern pl in an ancient setting.

open	Several Suns Mar, Apr, pm for charity, and by appointment
directions	SW84 50, from Truro take A39 Newquay road through St Erme, turn R to Trevella at end of Trispen
owners	The Hon. Mrs D. Verney & Ms R. Verney
address	Trevella, St Erme, Truro TR4 9BD
enquiries	T: 01872 510361 or 01872 510504 E: rosie@fsnet.co.uk
pronounced	treVELLa

MID-WEST

SW84 50

size	1.6ha/4a
soil	Lime-free
altitude	90m
aspect	In an AONB
rainfall	102–114cm/40–45in
temperature	Zone D

The house at Trevella is early 19th century, adjoining a farm, and curiously orientated so that the main door is rarely used, in favour of a back entrance through a conservatory. The side of the house faces the lawn and ha-ha, edged with belts of trees and rhododendrons. The main drive rises through lines of cherry trees before arriving at thin woodland near the house, similar to that leading out to the farm on the other side. Both are carpeted in the spring by a succession of snowdrops, primroses and bluebells, and other wild flowers, such as fritillaries, the open days being synchronized with their corresponding seasons. The high rhododendron and camellia hedges stem from plants brought by Mrs Verney upon moving from **Tregothnan** (60) in 1954, and the whole garden has been made since that date. The conservatory leads out on to the walled garden fringed with mixed borders, lush in springtime with various hostas, hellebores and euphorbias. By a parrotia – one of the few tree to have autumn colouring in Cornwall – the ornamental garden passes into a further section grasse over, but with an impressive line of five mature espalier apple trees. A door to the right leads out another lightly wooded area, which is being devel oped as a 'Millennium Garden' with camellias, shr roses, tree ferns, and rhododendrons – some of th 'grande' series.

open	Feb–May, Mon–Sun; Jun–Sep, Mon–Sat, am, pm
directions	SW91 47, on A390 Truro–St Austell road, 0.5ml E of Probus
owners	Mr A.M.J. Galsworthy
address	The Estate Office, Trewithen, Grampound Road, Truro TR2 4DD
enquiries	T: 01726 883647 F: 01726 882301 E: gardens@trewithen-estate.demon.co.uk www.trewithen gardens.co.uk
pronounced	treWITHen
EH	House: I

MID-WEST

SW91 47

EH	Gardens: II*
size	12ha/30a
soil	Lime-free
altitude	85–80m
aspect	S-facing
rainfall	102–114cm/40–45in
temperature	Zone C
	Nursery: wide-ranging, specializing in tender species

150

After a checkered family history, the old house at Trewithen, which had been enlarged for Thomas Hawkins by Thomas Edwards of Greenwich, was altered for Philip Hawkins in 1763–4 to designs by Sir Robert Taylor; but it was Thomas who was principally responsible for the major planting. The Record Office contains a notebook on 'The Care and Cultivation of Trees', written by him in 1745, and a 'Diary' written in 1757 by his father-in-law James Heywood. Woods were described to the south and south-west, which protected the house from the prevailing winds, and avenues radiating to the east and north. Thomas died in 1766, to be succeeded by his son, later Sir Christopher Hawkins, who was more interested in enlarging his estate than improving his grounds.

The 'Golden Age' began early in the 20th century after the succession of George Horace Johnstone in 1904, who first planted 100 hybrids of *Rhododendron arboreum*, two of which were named 'Alison Johnstone' (see page 122), after his wife, and 'Jack Skilton', after his gardener. Compulsory wartime tree-felling provided an opportunity to reshape and plant the lawn, which is now one of the outstanding features

of the garden. Trewithen is renowned for its uniqu collection of tender and rare plants. Among them Camellias, such as their own 'Elizabeth Johnstone' and 'Glenn's Orbit', and 'Donation', struck from th original at Borde Hill. G.H. Johnstone was also cel ebrated for his raising of daffodils, and his collect of magnolias, on which he was an authority. Amo the garden features are the walled garden with its lily pond and summerhouse, and the Cock Pit, a former quarry and now a rock garden. More rece platforms have been constructed for viewing this exceptional garden, which has 25 Champion trees

65 Trewithen

open	Apr–Sep, Sun, Tue, + bank holiday Mons, pm; other times by appointment
directions	SW91 39, from centre of Veryan on Portloe road, just past PO
owners	Graham & Brenda Salmon
address	Trist House, Veryan, Truro TR2 5QA
enquiries	T: 01872 501422 F: 01872 501211 E: grahamobs@a30.net www.Tristhouse.co.uk
EH	House: II

MID-WEST

SW91 39

size	2ha/5a
soil	Mostly lime-free
altitude	80–65m
aspect	NW-sloping, in an AONB
rainfall	89–102cm/35–40in
temperature	Zone C
	Plant sales

After the death of his father, Samuel Trist exchanged his Devon living with his successor, to become the third in the family to be instituted as vicar of Veryan. Since his mother continued to live in his father's mansion at Behan Park, he took over the vicarage from his brother Thomas, and in 1831 engaged Harrison, a London architect, to rebuild it, with a new lodge incorporating ornamental masonry from St Nun's Chapel in Grampound. He then commenced to lay out an elaborate garden at a cost of £1,000, which, in comparison with the £3,000 spent on the house was a vast sum. The present owners, however, fou the garden overgrown and in a somewhat dilapidated state, although gradually they have been abl to discover what still remains of the original. Ther is a Victorian rose arch and a Folly above the hous and in front three terraces ornamented with vases with a central pillar, which leads down to the lawr Their most astonishing discovery, however, lies to the west of the drive, where removal of undergrov revealed an extensive rockery, with a pool, and po sibly the remains of a grotto, which bears a strikin resemblance to similar rockwork at Hoole House, Chester, illustrated in the *Villa Gardener* of 1838. T remainder of the garden has been greatly develop since 1994 by the addition of mixed planting on t lawn below the terraces, alongside which has bee constructed a substantial rose pergola leading up to further bedding and plantations above. With the restoration of original features, and especially of the spectacular rockwork, this has established Tris House as the most important surviving parsonage garden in Cornwall.

66 Trist House

open	Daily, am, pm, entrance free
directions	SW82 45, entrance from St George's Road or by Crown Court
owners	Truro City Council
location	Edward Street, Truro
enquiries	T: 01872 274766 F: 01872 225572 E: info@truro.gov.uk www.truro.gov.uk

MID-WEST

SW82 45

size	Waterfall Gardens: 0.3ha/0.75a; Victoria Park: c.1.6ha/4a
soil	Lime-free
aspect	Steeply W-sloping
rainfall	102–114cm/40–45in
temperature	Zone C

During the development of Truro towards the en of the 19th century, the remaining freeholds of L Falmouth in the city were auctioned off in 1891, affording an opportunity for the purchase of a ple of land leading to the Tregear waterfall, near St George's Methodist Church, which was presented to the City in 1893. This was described as 'prettily laid out [by John Mitchinson, the Truro nursery-man] with flower beds, shrubs &c., and skirted by the Kenwyn stream, which [created] an ornament waterfall', from which the garden derived its nam Subsequently, new legislation made it possible fo the Council to provide pleasure gardens at pub-lic expense, and this resulted in the laying out of Victoria Park on the steep slopes above, between Waterfall Gardens and Castle Hill, now the site of Crown Court. This was opened, as a tablet record: in 1898 in commemoration of the 60th year of th reign of Queen Victoria. There were also at that ti an ornamental fountain, a bandstand, a drinking fountain presented in commemoration of the Queen's 81st birthday, an aquar-ium, and a caretaker's lodge in com-memoration of the coronation of King Edward VII. If the gardens are entered through the little gate and alleyway just below the Crown Court, the view opens on to a brilliant display of colourful bedding, leading down to the Victorian bandstand. The Parks' Department, which enters the 'Britain in Bloom' com-petition, have regularly received awards for their planting in this and other areas of the City. The railway viaduct towers over both gardens, offering a view of the Park that is a charming introduction to the city for the traveller entering the station from the east.

Grampound and Mevagissey

Grampound owed its initial success to its 'Great Bridge' (in Norman French *grand-pont*), which has been there since at least 1296, and was so-called because it was the main medieval highway crossing the then much broader River Fal, along the way from Truro to St Austell. Of three tanneries in the town in the 19th century, only one survived until recently, belonging to the Croggon family, whose houses, The Hollies and **Creed House** (72), have fine contemporary gardens. The quaintness of Mevagissey has long appealed to tourists, who are now additionally attracted to the no longer 'lost' gardens of **Heligan** (81), cultivated by the Tremayne family for some 300 years, and now themselves overshadowed by **The Eden Project** (73). But neither should detract from the colourful history of **Caerhays** (71) under the Trevanions (relatives of Lord Byron), or its present horticultural distinction.

(See gardens 71, 72, 94.)

St Austell, Lostwithiel and Fowey

St Austell owed its origin and increasing prosperity to mining – in two forms. Its early growth depended upon tin, particularly from the rich mine at Carclaze, which operated continuously from the 16th century until 1851; but though relatively ancient, the town never received a charter. Its greatest prosperity came in the late 18th century, as a result of experiments by the Wedgwoods to increase the strength and quality of their porcelain. From this time, St Austell was the centre of the china clay industry, allowing families like the Rashleighs of Fowey to create their country estates. Charles Rashleigh built the harbour at Charlestown to export clay, and landscaped **Menacuddle** (84), Prideaux House, and Duporth. However, **Tregrehan** (95), former seat of the Brodrugans, predates the town, and is opposite **Pine Lodge** (87) – probably our finest contemporary garden.

Lostwithiel is much older than St Austell, flourishing first as a ford at the high-water mark of the Fowey estuary; then under the protection of the royal dukes at Restormel Castle, and finally as the principal Stannary town, with the Court and 'Duchy Palace'. Eventually, it lost its place as a port to Fowey, whose natural harbour was the most important south-coast port in the 14th century. However, its steep valley sides precluded Fowey from expanding. **Headland** (75), a the mouth of the estuary, has been deve oped as a remarkable cliff garden, while **Boconnoc** (68), near Lostwithiel, is amon the greatest ancient Cornish estates.

(See gardens 68, 73, 74, 75, 76, 81, 83, 84, 87, 89, 91, 92, 95.)

Newquay, Padstow and Wadebridge

Newquay, Padstow and Wadebridge, the three focal points in the north, although of differing origins, share a common history as fishing ports. This was always the function of Newquay. Padstow grew up around the monastery of St Petroc.

Grampound
Mevagissey
St Austell
Lostwithiel
Fowey
Newquay
Padstow
Wadebridge
Bodmin

4 MID-EAST

wide, sandy estuary was ideal for the
ne fishing of pilchards, which provided
:ular employment and prosperity. The
gin and history of Wadebridge is en-
sulated in its name – 'Wade', an early
dieval low-tide crossing of the Camel.
Newquay boasted no great houses
til the Regency craving for the sea air
a few wealthy landowners to set up
rine residences. But **Trenance Gardens**
) are a fine example of a public park.
wever, there are ancient and great
ses in the vicinity, especially **Trerice**
), and **Tresillian House** (98). Central to
dstow is **Prideaux Place** (90), dominat-
the town. Yet exposure of the north
ast to the elements has been a deterrent
the creation of large gardens, and only
e – **Long Cross** (80) – is in the gazetteer.
(See gardens 77, 80, 90, 96, 97, 98.)

dmin

dmin is the only town in Cornwall
ntioned in the 'Domesday Book',
ere it was recorded that the Canons of

St Petroc owned 68 houses and a market,
making it probably the most populous
place in the county. When it received its
charter in the 13th century, the strong
religious life around the monastery sus-
tained the markets and fairs that brought
great wealth. After a relative decline in
the 17th and 18th centuries, Bodmin
re-emerged in the 19th century as a
route centre. Its eventual loss of status
may have been due in part to a refusal to
allow the railway into the town. In 1988
the transfer of the Law Courts to Truro,
which already held the County Hall and
Cathedral, spelt the end for Bodmin as
the County Town. Over the centuries,
Cornwall's centre of gravity moved from
Launceston, to Bodmin, and finally to
Truro, which is truly central. A number of
important historic gardens are grouped
around Bodmin, including that of the Robartes family at **Lanhydrock** (79), and of
Sir William Molesworth at **Pencarrow** (86).
*(See gardens 69, 70, 78, 79, 82, 85, 86,
88, 93.)*

MID-EAST

SX14 60

158

The Domesday manor of Boconnoc has a long an distinguished history, with the deer park – license in 1381 – being the only medieval park in Cornwa to have survived to the present day. The estate was purchased in 1717 by Thomas Pitt, Governor of Madras, from the proceeds of his sale of the 'Pitt Diamond'. His grandson, William 1st Earl of Chatham, was a patron of 'Capability Brown' and amateur landscaper, who may have influenced his brother Thomas in 'improving' his estate. Thomas son, the 2nd Baron Camelford, was an exponent c the 'picturesque' style, and added his contribution the landscape, so that Gilbert, in his *Historical Surv* (1822), wrote that 'the pleasing scenery of nature viewed in all its different attitudes, whilst the deco tions of art are lost to the eye, and almost to the in agination'. William Mason, the celebrated poet of *English Garden* (1772), is reported to have remarke that the River Lerryn flowing through Boconnoc 'v

68 Boconnoc

uch handsomer nymph than his Not-
hamshire Ligea, and had he been earlier
uainted with her charms, should certainly
e occupied her place in his poem'. Dur-
the 19th century, a Pinetum was added,
various plantings of beech and conifers
e made. The house, now being restored,
s upon a platform below the rock face on
ch the church stands. There are orna-
tal gardens on this level, with a fountain,
d, dovecote, and bath-house. However,
greatest beauty of Boconnoc lies in its
scape – the wooded slopes; the lake
restored; the valley of the Lerryn, and
ong drive passing the obelisk erected in
1, framed by two classical shrines. This
historic site, where Charles I made his
dquarters during the Civil War.

open	Some Suns May, Jul, pm, and by appointment
directions	SX03 65, turn at Pressingol Pottery (A30) signposted Nanstallon, L at crossroads signposted Hoopers Bridge, then sharp R
owners	P.M. & W.M. Appleton
address	Bodwannick Manor, Nanstallon, Bodmin PL30 5LN
enquiries	T: 01208 831427
pronounced	bodWANnick
EH	House

MID-EAST

SX03 65

size	0.6ha/1.5a
soil	Lime-free
altitude	60m
rainfall	114–127cm/45–50in
temperature	Zone E

A manor dating from the 12th century, the present old and romantic house with a slate-floored veran dah and rough-hewn granite pillars was built on the original site, with the 'Bodwannick Cross' in the centre of the front lawn. To the left of the entrance drive is the vegetable garden, below which is a wide grass pathway with large rhododendrons on the left, and a rose bed on the right. Above this bed is a long pergola covered with a white wiste ria, forming the lower boundary of the vegetable garden. Along another side are three rose arches. The pathway leads out into a grassed area where a stone circle has been set up using boulders from an ancient mine. Upon returning along the upper side of the kitchen garden, the path down to the house passes between rockwork planted with hostas and other herbaceous plants. The house and its garden is separate, on the right of the approach, entered between two small beds of dwarf conifers. There i a conservatory with an array of streptocarpus, and a wall supporting several pots of begonias, flanked by an orange and lemon tree. The garden is richly planted, especially on the rising ground above a pond, fringed with acers, astilbe, ornamental grass es and a conifer. A collection of some 50 daffodils contrasts with the rhododendrons and camellias in the springtime. This is a varied and interesting garden with an aura of antiquity. In 2005 it won the TSW Garden of the Year competition.

69 Bodwannick Manor

open	One Sun in May and by appointment in May and Jun, pm
directions	SX09 75, from Bodmin take B3266. Turn R to St Breward. Cross Wenford Bridge. Take R fork at Millennium Stone. Garden is 0.5ml on L
owners	Jackie & George Greengrass
address	Bolts Quarry Farm, Penvorder Lane, St Breward, Bodmin PL30 4NY
enquiries	T: 01208 851592 E: boltsfarm@ ukonline.co.uk www.boltsfarm.co.uk

MID-EAST

SX09 75 —

size	1.6ha/4a in 6.9ha/17a smallholding
soil	Acid
altitude	150m
aspect	E, in an AGLV
rainfall	102–114cm/40–45in
temperature	Zone E
	Plant sales

This garden is part of a smallholding perched on very of edge of Bodmin Moor. The house is tucke into the lee of the high ground, and the land spre out across the hillside into more exposed areas, w wide views over the countryside as far as the sea. Jackie and George Greengrass have been working the garden since 2001, and have made full use of natural advantages of the site. Behind the house an area of small, private spaces. Huge granite blc have been built into a massive wall, curving roun echo the contours of the hillside. Different viewpc reveal a range of carefully planned vistas through the planting, and granite standing stones lend ext height and form. A winding path leads through cc lections of rhododendrons and azaleas that give a brilliant range of spring colours. Later in the year a long, herbaceous border takes precedence, and by late summer hardy geraniums and monkshooc cover the stonework. The sand school for the hors

70 Bolts Quarry Farm

ls to the outer parts of
garden. Areas cleared of
rgrown scrub are now cov-
l in bluebells in season,
the underlying character
ne land is revealed by old
ge lines, solid stone walls,
the twisted boughs of an
ient oak tree. A natural
d provides a shady water
ure, below which a boggy
a is ideal for gunnera and
nthus. Even the old quarry
been utilized – as an
l area for the occasional
door performance.

open	Garden: mid-Feb–end summer, incl bank holidays, daily am, pm; free to RHS members mid-Feb–mid Mar. House: mid-Mar–May, Mon–Fri, pm.
directions	SW97 41, Mevagissey turn on A390 E of Grampound; signed
owner	Julian Williams
address	Estate Office, Gorran, St Austell PL26 6LY
enquiries	T: 01872 501310 F: 01872 501870 E: estateoffice@ caerhays.co.uk www.caerhays.co.uk
pronounced	C'RAZE
EH	House: I; many garden features I and II

MID-EAST

SW97 41

EH	Gardens: II*
size	24ha/60a
soil	Lime-free
altitude	70m–sea; house 25m
aspect	NE-, N-, and E-sloping, in an AONB
rainfall	89–102cm/35–40in
temperature	Zone C
NC	Magnolias
	Plant sales

From about 1379 Caerhays belonged to the Trevanions, later related to Lord Byron. Between 1805 and 1807 John Bettesworth Trevanion engaged the celebrated John Nash to build the present Castle. Described as a 'folly', it certainly bankrupted the Trevanions. It then lay unfinished and derelict until purchased in 1854 by Michael Williams of Scorrier (25), whose grandson, J.C. Williams, may be regarded as the founder of the great reputation of Caerhays: a plantsman's garden of national, perhaps international importance. He sponsored or contributed to several plant-hunting expeditions, notably those of Forrest, Wilson, Farrer and Kingdon Ward, and the gardens reflect their discoveries of rhododendrons, azaleas, camellias and magnolias. Other collections were made of hydrangeas, lithocarpus and nothofagus. Seeds from these expeditions were sent back to the contributors, and were propagated and planted in the grounds above the Castle. Many of these introduced specimens and varieties flowered for the first time at Caerhays. J.C. Williams also interested himself in breeding hybrids, of which 12 appear in the *Register* – 'Blue Tit', 'Humming Bird', 'Yellow Hammer', and 'Royal Flush' being best known. Of equal, or perhaps greater fame

the camellia crosses made
·een *Camellia japonica* and *sal-*
·is, which have become known
·*illiamsii* camellias. Among
·e are 'J.C. Williams' and 'Mary
·stian', named after J.C. and
·wife, and 'Charles Michael',
·ed after his gardener. In 1893,
·Williams also began to raise
·odils. In a recent survey of
·*npion Trees*, 13 were recorded
··, to which a further nine may
·dded. For these and many
··r reasons, Caerhays may justly
·egarded as the most important
·tsman's garden in Cornwall.

71 Caerhays Castle Gardens

open	Feb–Oct, daily, am, pm
directions	SW93 47, from centre of Grampound on A390, take road signed to Creed. After 1ml turn L opposite Creed Church, garden on L
owners	Mr & Mrs William Croggon
address	Creed House, Creed, Grampound, Truro TR2 4SL
enquiries	T: 01872 530372

MID-EAST

SW93 47

size	2ha/5a
soil	Lime-free
altitude	35m
aspect	W-sloping
rainfall	102–114cm/40–45in
temperature	Zone D
	Plant sales

Formerly the rectory of the parish of St Crida, Creed House was built around 1730, with its extensive grounds sloping westwards. When the Croggons arrived in 1974, the garden was totally overgrown, and took them about ten years to bring back into shape enough to begin serious planting. There is a range of buildings behind the house, where various forms of garden are being created. A derelict summerhouse was restored in 1977. The stables have two cobbled areas in front, the lower of which is concave, and was probably intended as a carriage-wash. To the rear, the walled garden, at first used for vegetables, has been lawned, and contrasting herbaceous borders are being developed. Rising from this lawn are steps to the top woodland of some 2.5 acres (1ha) planted with indigenous trees. The west front of the house, with borders and a terrace, looks down on to a large, flat lawn, probably originally intended for bowls or croquet. This drops to the naturally sloping lawn beyond, the bank planted with spring bulbs. The garden principally consists of a deep belt, presenting from the house a rich tapestry of colour and texture, through which wind many walks among planta- tions of trees with underplanting of shrubs. Here are a group of calocedrus and an acer mod on those at Westonbirt. A large pond has a terrac which leads into a bog garden planted with sku cabbage, candelabra primulas and ferns. The ob in the planting of the walks has been not only to variety, but to open vistas, some looking out ove surrounding countryside, others looking inwards paths lit by broken sunlight.

open	Daily, excl 24, 25 Dec, am, pm
directions	SX04 54, follow brown signs from A30 and A390
owner	The Eden Trust
address	The Eden Project, Bodelva, St Austell PL24 2SG
enquiries	T: 01726 811911 F: 01726 811912 E: esteel@ edenproject.com www.edenproject.com

MID-EAST

SX04 54

size	Extensive former china-clay pit, c.20ha/50a
soil	Composted
altitude	105m
rainfall	114–127cm/45–50in
temperature	Zone E
	Plant centre

Cornwall's major tourist attraction, and the first port of call for almost every visitor to the county, the Eden Project opened in 2001. The sight of the vast 'biomes', like giant soap bubbles, is the first cause of astonishment; the second, upon entering them, is the virtuosity of the engineering that has made all this possible. The whole complex occupies a vast pit resulting from the commercial extraction of china clay – a medium in itself inhospitable to plant life, but which has been made fertile by composting. The larger biome represents the humid tropics, planted with many tropical varieties, including fully-grown trees, around a grand water feature pouring down over the cliff side. To maintain humidity, there is a regular emission of mist, which further enhances the impression of a 'rain forest'. The smaller biome represents the warm temperate, or Mediterranean zone, and its planting includes olives, grape vines, citrus fruits, agaves, and other succulents, some of which grow outdoors in Cornwall at gardens such as **Lamorran House** (49) on the mainland, and the **Abbey Gardens** (1) on Tresco. A third

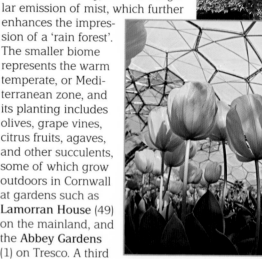

biome is in prospect, to represent the arid or desert zone. The surrounding grounds, which are extensive, are landscaped with large-scale designs and sculptures to suit the great size of the arena, which also used for a variety of events and concerts. Eden is described as a 'Project', since its ultimate purpose is not so much entertainment as education. Its aim has been to replace the formality of outdated botanic gardens, by promulgating its central message – that humanity is dependent upon the plant world. For this reason, alongside the visitor attractions, shops and plant sales, there are exhibitions and talks, and ancillary study and training centres.

73 The Eden Project

SW55 88, from A30 take Summercourt exit. At traffic lights take lane beside corner shop. After 0.5ml garden is on L

Andrew & Angela Bailey

Goenrounsen House, Carnego Lane, Summercourt, Newquay TR8 5BQ

T: 01872 510604

GUNrounsen

House: II

D-EAST

W55 88

4.8ha/12a set in 6.1ha/15a

Acid

100m

SE

89–102cm/35–40in

Zone D

When Andrew and Angela Bailey moved into Goenrounsen in 1999, they took on a residence in a sorry state, and a surrounding garden once well planted with camellias and magnolias but now in need of restoration. Since then, not only have they renovated the house and regenerated the existing lawns and shrubberies, but they have used the adjoining land to create a series of new gardens. A major undertaking has been the silver birch copse planted as a central feature in an arboretum, surrounded by young specimen trees such as *Paulownia tomentosa*, *Magnolia sprengeri*, *Acer palmatum*, *Cedrus deodara* 'Aurea', and even a *Metasequoia glyptostroboides* – the Dawn redwood. As these trees mature, they will form a truly impressive sight. A path leads down to a sizeable wildlife pond created out of a swampy meadow. Already fringed with magnificent velvety bulrushes, it gains colour from irises, water lilies and water hyacinths. Gunnera grows on an island, and donated willow cuttings are forming a plantation on one side. A deep Cornish lane borde by old oak trees contains an impressive avenue of young tree ferns leading to a gazebo. Beyond lie a orchard and a wild-flower meadow. Nearer the ho is the hydrangea garden, home to an astonishing 800 individual plants in about 40 different varietie The paniculata varieties have been placed at the back, as they will be allowed to attain their full he of about 5m (15 ft). Strategically placed catalpas g immediate height while the garden matures.

74 Goenrounsen

open	May–Aug, Thu pm
directions	SX12 50, by ferry from Fowey + 10-min walk along West Street and up Battery Lane. By car follow signs to Polruan on E side of estuary, ignore 1st car-park, turn L and park in 2nd car-park (overlooking harbour), turn L (on foot) down St Saviour's Hill
owner	Mrs Jean Hill
address	Headland, Battery Lane, Polruan-by-Fowey PL23 1PW
enquiries	T: 01726 870243

MID-EAST

SX12 50

size	0.5ha/1.25a
soil	Neutral
aspect	W-sloping, 30m to sea, in an AONB
rainfall	89–102cm/35–40in
temperature	Zone D

Headland Garden was first laid out when the hou[se] was built between 1900 and 1915 in a quarry, wh[ere] much topsoil must have been brought in before planting. Jean and John Hill bought the house in 1974, not for the garden, but as a holiday home. [...] down the years it has attracted widespread attenti[on] from the media, and was once the setting for a fil[m.] The garden is perched high on a cliff, exposed to [the] sea and wind on three sides. There is a successful vegetable garden at the top of a precipitous drop [to] a small cove below, which is accessible down step[s.] The walls, paths and arches, which blend with the natural slates, were constructed by John Hill and Peter Ball. Shelter, which is essential, was from th[e] outset provided by the Monterey Pine (*Pinus radia[ta*], most now past their best, but with new ones grow[-] ing to the same height. Hawthorn and Mountain [Ash] have proved successful, although distorted, and a[lso] olearia and the *Genista* 'Porlock'; lower hedges of escallonia, *Hippophae rhamnoides*, and euonymou[s] moulded into the shape of the rock provide shelte[r,] behind them even for exotics such as agaves, aloe[s,] aeoniums, lampranthus, the Hottentot Fig, *Carpro-botus edulis*, and also *Aptenia cordifolia* from Israe[l.] Headland has been open for many years for chari[ty,] and in 2000 received an award from the RNLI for raising a total of £22,000. However, the garden ha[s] qualities that will appeal to many, whether or not they wish to support the RNLI.

75 Headland Garden

open	Mid-Mar–Oct, daily, am, pm
directions	SX08 55, off A390, take B3269 signed Fowey, within 200yd fork R signed Treesmill and follow signs
owners	Tricia Howard
address	Hidden Valley, Treesmill, nr Par PL24 2TU
enquiries	T: 01208 873225 E: hiddenvalley gardens:yahoo.co.uk www.hiddenvalley gardens.co.uk

MID-EAST

SX08 55

size	Medium
soil	Lime-free
altitude	From 25m
aspect	S-facing
rainfall	102–114cm/40–45in
temperature	Zone D
	Nursery: specializes in herbaceous and cottage plants

The Howard family moved in 1999 from Northern Yorkshire to the very different climate of Cornwall, bringing with them over 1,000 plants, with the intention of setting up a garden and nursery on a site that had been run as a soft-fruit small-holding. The house is a converted stone barn, with the entrance gravelled and formally planted with raised beds. Below the nursery is a long bed of 'hot' colours and purple foliage, leading down to a pool fed by a stream running through woodland, which has yet to be developed. To the side of the house are two large rectangular beds with four golden yews, which will eventually be trimmed into cones. Around the greenhouse are stock beds, and the beginning of a Mediterranean garden with cistus, rosemary, myrtle, lavender, and *Convolvulus sabatius*. This garden is still in its infancy, but has much to offer, and great potential.

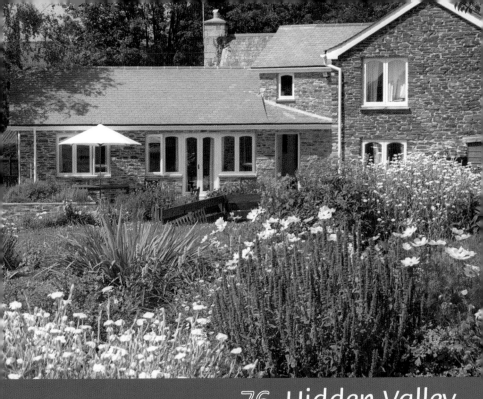

76 Hidden Valley Gardens & Nurseries

open	Daily, excl 25 Dec– 1 Jan, am, pm
directions	SW87 66, in centre of village
owners	Rob & Stella Hore
address	The Japanese Garden & Bonsai Nursery, St Mawgan, Newquay TR8 4ET
enquiries	T: 01637 860116 F: 01637 860887 E: rob@thebonsai nursery.com www.thebonsai nursery.com

MID-EAST
SW87 66

size	0.6ha/1.5a
soil	Lime-free
aspect	In an AGLV
rainfall	102–114cm/40–45in
temperature	Zone D
	Nursery: specializes in bonsai and Japanese garden plants

The idea for a Japanese Garden began in 1988, when Robert Hore and his wife Stella returned to native Cornwall from London. The chosen site wa a run-down smallholding, which required clearin The inspiration came from the unexpected gift of bonsai, which aroused an enthusiasm issuing in determination to do something about it. The gard does not necessarily follow orthodox rules precis although it is the result of much study, and has v the approval of Japanese visitors. The focal point the tea house, representing a traditional Japanes ceremony, whose balcony overlooks the beautiful pond and waterfall. Another characteristic feature is the Zen garden of tranquillity, which is without plants, and consists solely of carefully placed roc on sand brought to life daily by raking. Plants do nonetheless play an important part, especially the conifers, bamboos, camellias and acers. These br colour and texture to the planting, the vibrant col of the springtime azaleas contrasting with the dy ing hues of the acers in autumn. The garden first opened to the public in 1997, when its appearanc of maturity belied the relatively short period of it creation. This was made possible by in-corporating existing mature trees, and by importing well-weathered stone.

The Bonsai Nursery forms an integral part of the whole concept – indeed, the garden has grown out of the nursery, rather than, as is often the case, being merely an added extra. Japanese gar-dens are fashionable, although often little more than a corner of an English garden with a pond, a bridge, a lantern and an acer. A visit to this garden will induce the authentic atmosphere of the real thing.

77 The Japanese Garden & Bonsai Nursery

open	One Sun Aug, pm
directions	SX07 67, N side of town, 100yd up hill from Westberry Hotel
owners	Dr & Mrs M.S. Stead
address	Kingberry, 38 Rhind Street, Bodmin PL31 2EL
enquiries	See NGS annual yellow book or www.ngs.org.uk

MID-EAST

SX07 67

size	0.4ha/1a
soil	Alkaline
rainfall	114–127cm/45–50in
temperature	Zone D
	Plant sales

The narrow entrance from the street belies the ex and richness of the garden beyond. The old hous was built in 1830, facing south at a right angle to the road. When the present owners arrived in 199 the grounds were principally given over to marke gardening and fruit. The walls of the house at the entrance are still covered with a 100-year-old pea tree bearing tiny, though sweet fruit. The garden the front is lawned, with wide herbaceous border mixed colours, influenced by combinations seen **Bosvigo** (39). The far side of the house is mostly en up by a fine conservatory, with two puyas in p by the door, which looks out over a long lawn wit serpentine herbaceous border along the wall of tl remaining orchard, towards a white 'flowered' *Co kousa chinensis* – the flowers in fact being bracts; yellow-foliaged *Robinia pseudoacacia* 'Frisia', and the silver 'Weeping Pear' *Pyrus salicifolia*, providir an interesting association of colour and form. To left a long yew hedge divides the lawn from a 'Se Garden'. Within an alcove formed in this hedge is striking sculptured head designed by a member c the Shona tribe in 1997 and brought from Zimba- bwe. The 'Secret Garden' is entered at the end of hedge via a terrace with a bench and small shed covered by a Kiwi Fruit *Actinidia chinen- sis*. The theme of this formal garden is leaf- shape and texture rather than flowers, using such plants as rodgersia, phormiums, ferns and grasses. A gravel path runs the whole length of the garden, broken in the centre with a crossing marked by a *Catalpa bignon- ioides purpura*, with a small pond to the right. This is a garden of peaceful luxuriance.

open	Daily, am, pm; house mid-Mar–end Oct, Tue–Sun + bank holiday Mons, am, pm
directions	SX08 63, follow brown signs, on B3268
owner	NT
address	Lanhydrock, Bodmin PL30 5AD
enquiries	T: 01208 265950 F: 01208 265959 E: lanhydrock@ nationaltrust.org.uk www.nationaltrust .org.uk
pronounced	lanHIGHdrock
EH	House, church, gatehouse, gateway, walls at E entrance: I; many garden features II* and II

MID-EAST

SX08 63

EH	Garden, parkland: II*
size	10ha/25a
soil	Lime-free (pH 4.5), good medium loam
altitude	130–100m
aspect	E-sloping, in a SAGLV
rainfall	127–152cm/50–60in
temperature	Zone E
	Plant centre

Lanhydrock has had a chequered history since John Robartes built his house in 1635–42, on four sides of an inner court, with a long avenue of sycamores leading up to the gatehouse. In 1758 his successor, following the fashion for bringing the lawn right up to the house, demolished the east wing of the house, opening up the inner court, and leaving the gatehouse isolated and disconnected. He also added a double row of beech trees on each side of the sycamore avenue, and extended the woodland. In the mid-19th century, Thomas James Agar inherited the property. He assumed the name Robartes, and used his great wealth, derived from mining, to improve his estate. In 1857 the fashionable architect George Gilbert Scott, a renowned Gothicist, was employed to extend the ancient dwelling, and reincorporate the gatehouse in the formal gardens beside and in front of the house, which we see today. The Higher Garden behind the house was laid out as a shrubbery at about this time. After a disastrous fire in 1881, the restoration was put in the hands of Richard Coad, of Liskeard, formerly from Scott's office. The seventh Lord Clifden, who inherited the estate in 1930, began replanting the slopes to the rear with ornamental trees and shrubs more in line with current trends than the old Victorian shrubberies. The thatched gardener's cottage, last occupied in 1885, was made a feature, and is now a shelter. He also purchased the splendid bronze urns, designed by Louis Ballin, goldsmith to Louis XIV. Lanhydrock was donated to the National Trust 1953, and the Trust has added two quadrants to the semi-circular herbaceous border planted in 1914.

79 Lanhydrock

open	Daily, am, pm
directions	SW98 79, turning N off B3314 either at Endellion, or through Trelights, arrives at Long Cross in about 1ml
owner	James Bishop
address	Long Cross Hotel, Trelights, Port Isaac PL29 3TF
enquiries	T: 01208 880243 F: 01208 880560 E: info@longcross hotel.co.uk www.longcross hotel.co.uk

MID-EAST

SX98 79

size	1.2ha/3a
soil	Neutral
altitude	100m
aspect	In an AONB
rainfall	89–102cm/35–40in
temperature	Zone D

The house was built around 1900, and is named after the ancient stone cross at the crossroads immediately opposite the north-east gate entranc The garden was designed by the then owner, a Ca Allerdyce, with the help of several local gardeners Subsequently, it fell into decay, although it was sti possible to discern the original plan. During the 1980s the then owners began a restoration, which has been continued by their successors. The maze like nature of the garden might at first sight appea puzzling, until it is recognized that the prevalence of gales from the north coast required both shelte and specialized planting. Several of the Monterey Pines planted as a shelterbelt still survive, and the hedges of escallonia and olearia are salt-tolerant. Below the level of the hedges, it is possible for the more normal species to thrive, and several of the original plants – Welsh poppies, aquilegias and feverfew – have regenerated and self-seeded. Tod the borders are again ablaze with herbaceous pla such as lysimachia, lilies, and geraniums. Herbs have become a speciality. The central feature of the garden is an 'ornamental water', with an islan decorated with four classical pillars, a statue, and cordylines. Nearby is a 'Mount', opening up a view of the coast, from which at night the lighthouses of Trevose, Hartland and Lundy may be seen. Hidden among the trees is a folly castle from the original garden, and more prominently a modern reproduction dovecote. Long Cross garden is associated with an hotel, which also operates as a seasonal bar and restaurant.

open	Daily, excl 24, 25 Dec, am, pm; house private
directions	SW99 46, B3273 from St Austell signposted Mevagissey and follow signs
contact	Mr Henry Cavender
address	Mr Henry Cavender, Heligan, Pentewan, St Austell PL26 6EN
enquiries	T: 01726 845100 F: 01726 845101 E: info@heligan.com www.heligan.com
pronounced	heLIGan, often anglicized to HELigan
EH	House: separate II; kitchen garden walls II

MID-EAST

SW99 46

EH	Gardens: II
size	81ha/200a
soil	Lime-free
altitude	95–25m, house 80m
aspect	S- and SE-sloping, in an AONB
rainfall	102–114cm/40–45in
temperature	Zone D
	Plant centre

The effect of two world wars and social change spelt the end of most great estates. To prevent their total disappearance, in the 1960s the National Trust began to restore gardens, such as **Glendurgan** (43), **Trelissick** (61) and **Trengwainton** (30), as distinct from houses. They were followed by private entrepreneurs, such as Maj. Tony Hibbert at **Trebah** (58). This movement inspired Tim Smit to restore the 'lost' garden of the Tremayne family at Heligan. Both the house and garden had a long history – a quite elaborate, formal garden was swept away in the late 18th century, to be replaced by the landscape seen toda[y]. The delapidated walled garden with its glasshouse[s] for grapes, peaches and even bananas, and its pits for pineapples, were the first to be restored, with a working kitchen and flower garden. This was followed by a large, organic vegetable garden, using techniques pioneered by John Harris in the Victori[an] walled garden at **Tresillian House** (98). Large esta[tes] had big families, armies of servants, and regiment[s] of outside workers to feed, and the surplus went to market. The valley, or 'Japanese Garden', now the 'Jungle', and so called from the origin of many of [its] plants, was tackled next. There was a ravine as we[ll] as a rock garden, and a small 'Italian' garden more reminiscent of household gardens in Pompeii than the elaborate statuary and fountain gardens of the Tivoli. Mrs Tremayne planted an 'old-fashioned' he[r]baceous border in a walled garden. All of these an[d] more were restored to recreate the atmosphere of [a] typical 19th-century garden. The publicity given to Heligan has led to a welcome increase in enthusias[m] for visiting historic gardens, and encouraged furthe[r] revivals, such as that at **Trevarno** (32).

184

open	Apr–Sep, Sun, am, pm
directions	SX11 75, on Bodmin Moor take turning to St Breward off A30 with a cattle grid at the crossroad opposite turning to Temple, and continue 1m bearing R to Bradford. Sculpture Garden is on L
owner	Ms Sheila Holland
address	Lower Bradford, Blisland, Bodmin PL30 4LF
enquiries	T: 01208 850195 www.sculpturegarden. mysite.freeserve.com

MID-EAST

SX11 75 ___

size	1ha/2.4a
soil	Lime-free
altitude	217m
aspect	In a SAGLV
rainfall	102–114cm/40–45in
temperature	Zone E

This is a garden snatched from the open moorlan although not itself a moorland garden. When She Holland arrived here in 1986, this was no more t a flat field. Since then, she has been steadily plar ing such trees as took her fancy, protected from t winds by an inconspicuous belt of conifers. After son had moved to town, with advancing years, w nature began to take over, but following his retur unwelcome intruders such as brambles are being banished. The garden is entered through a court- yard where the sculptures are on view, together v plants for sale. A path leads up to the garden exp ing a depression, excavated to relieve the flatness the site, with paths running around the perimete and a central 'island' surmounted with rockwork. wild and semi-wild plants growing here are gene small, but all around rise the tall trees. The progr sive stages of planting have resulted in these and the underlying shrubs being so placed that they a viewed in the round, for this is not a woodland, b varied and fascinating personal collection, plante be admired. One enthusiasm has been for eucaly many not found in Cornish nurseries – and perha not even in many gardens – but which, year by y have been introduced from specialist nurseries. W their striking bark and strange leaves, they contra with our more familiar species. This is not a manicured garden; rough paths wind through grassland rich in spring with wild flowers – campion, primros- es and foxgloves – with here and there the occasional sculpture. During the season there are also rhododendrons and magnolias in bloom, but this should not deter tree-lovers at other seasons, whose visits will be equally well rewarded. The website contains a map giving directions.

82 Lower Bradford Wilderness Sculpture Garden

open	Apr–Oct, Sun–Wed, am, pm
directions	SX07 54, leave A390 at St Blazey traffic lights, then take first L over level crossing. Garden 800yd on L
owner	Mrs Judith Stephens
address	Marsh Villa, St Andrews Road, Par, St Austell PL24 2LU
enquiries	T: 01726 815920

MID-EAST

SX07 54

size	1.2ha/3a
soil	In-filled
altitude	River level
aspect	114–127cm/45–50in
temperature	Zone D
	Plant sales

The gardens at Marsh Villa have been created ou of a former tidal creek, made famous by Daphne du Maurier in her novel *House on the Strand*. It ha taken 17 years for the marshland to be consolida chiefly with waste soil of no great quality, which, however, belies the great interest and beauty of the garden. The main garden is long and relative narrow, ending in natural marsh that is a haven for wildlife. Paths wander through areas variousl planted with trees, and underplanted with shrubs and the occasional herbaceous border. As one str through the various glades, a catalpa and huge contorted willow catch the eye, and a *Cornus kou* with white bracts; then a paulownia; the evergre late-flowering hoheria, followed by the parrotia, of the few trees to colour well in Cornwall. There both forms of drimys; a clerodendron, and a Juda tree – a list that merely whets the appetite, rather than exhausts the many other varieties to be seer At the end of these walks are two areas hedged v escallonia. The first screens a large, natural pond with water-lilies and hovering dragonflies, overlooked by a summerhouse. The second, by way of contrast, encloses a formal garden with two full herbaceous borders running the length of each side, and a third island bed in the centre be- tween them. These have each been expertly and harmoniously planted with contrasting colour schemes. This is a most rewarding garden to visit, of great variety and quality.

83 Marsh Villa Gardens

Menacuddle was celebrated for its artificial waterfall, emanating from a well in the floor of the ruined chapel or baptistry, the waters of which 'roll through a narrow dell, darkened with leafage, and strewed with enormous rocks' to flow away under Menacuddle bridge. Gilbert, in his *Historical Survey*, described the scene in 1822 after the garden had been purchased and restored by Charles Rashleigh:

> There is a variety of intricate walks carried through the inclosure; also ponds, stored with fish of gold and silver hues. The upper walks stretch over the steep acclivities, in zig-zag directions, accompanied by rustic seats, formed of rough blocks of wood, covered with moss, and entwined with ivy. Opposite a rustic building called the Hermitage, stands a pedestal, capped with an urn, bearing a profile likeness of the late earl of Mount Edgcumbe.

The grounds later fell into decay, but were restored by Sir Charles Sawle in memory of his son, who was killed in the First World War, and presented to the local authorities as public gardens. Today they have again regressed, but may still be relish by those with an appetite for the eerie isolation o place, echoing with the rush of tumbling waters.

84 Menacuddle

open	Apr–Sep, daily, excl Wed, am, pm
directions	SX06 71, access from A30 1ml N of Bodmin, or from B3266 Bodmin–Camelford road
owners	Mr & Mrs R.D. Whurr
address	The Old Mill Herbary, Helland Bridge, Bodmin PL30 4QR
enquiries	T: 01208 841206 E: oldmillherbary@ aol.com www.oldmillherbary. co.uk

MID-EAST

SX06 71

size	2ha/5a
soil	Neutral to acid
altitude	41m
aspect	S-facing, in an AONB, SAGLV, SSSI, SAC
rainfall	102–114cm/40–45in
temperature	Zone E
	Plant sales

Formerly part of the ancient Colquite Estate, the Old Mill is situated alongside the venerable Helland Bridge, the only bridge in the Camel valley, other than that at Wadebridge, to survive the 'Great Flood' of 1847. In the mid-17th century there was a 1-acre (0.4ha) hop yard here, and by 1775 an herb garden and orchard. The corn and saw mill, demolished c. 1939, were in use until the mid-1930s, run from a leat fed by a natural stream, supplemented in summer by the river. The semi-wild garden has been created entirely by the owners since 1984, and opened to the public in 1986. The leat has been cleaned and restored to pass beneath a renovated granite clapper bridge, which now feeds natural bog and water gardens, set around an unabashed Greek/Roman fertility theme. Relics, including granite troughs and mushrooms, and a large granite cider press – now a fountain – may be seen in the garden, and a large variety of named, planted displays of culinary, medicinal and aromatic herbs. There are unusual and rare species of seasonal wild flowers, bamboos, shrubs and climbers; a 1.75-acre (0.7ha) riverside lawned arboretum, with over 40 named and unusual trees; a terraced camomile lawn, and a patio pond with aquatics. The Old Mill Herbary attracts many wh are interested, or professionally involved, in kind subjects, and the garden abounds in birds, butte and insects, with the occasional otter. The woodl walks in springtime are carpeted with daffodils, I bells and wood anemones, and later with ferns.

85 The Old Mill Herbary

open	Mar–Oct, daily am, pm; house, etc from Apr, Sun–Thu
directions	SX04 71, signed off A389 and B3266
owners	Molesworth-St Aubyn family
address	Pencarrow, Washaway, Bodmin PL30 3AG
enquiries	T: 01208 841369 F: 01208 841722 E: info@pencarrow. co.uk www.pencarrow.co.uk
pronounced	penCARRo, as in arrow
EH	House: II; fountain, grotto, rock garden, garden house, walled kitchen garden, ice-house, each II

MID-EAST

SX04 71

EH	Gardens: II*
size	Size 20ha/50a
soil	Lime-free
altitude	75–150m
aspect	House S-facing
rainfall	102–114cm/40–45in
temperature	Zone E
	Plant centre

Once a Domesday manor, Pencarrow was remodelled in about 1844 by George Wightwick for Sir William Molesworth, who as Chief Commissioner of Works had arranged for the opening to the public of Kew Gardens. His popularity with his constituents led to their assisting him in laying out his grounds between his political activities. First, he created the elaborate, semi-elliptical Italian Garden, the central fountain copied from that in the Piazza Navonna in Rome. Corbett, his gardener, on the eastern side simulated a moorland rock-strewn slope, with a cave and grotto. These innovations were followed by planting the main, mile-long (1.6km) drive with trees raised from seed obtained from the mid-century plant hunters, such as William Lobb, Sir Joseph Hooker, and David Douglas, and from Veitch's nursery in Exeter. His last task was to plant up the Green Drive leading to the Camelford Gate; an American Garden of conifers; and rhododendrons and some camellias, under a canopy of beech and elm. Before his death in 1855, Sir William was able to boast that he had planted a specimen of every conifer, save ten, capable of growing in the Cornish climate. The work of planting was continued by his sister, Mrs Ford. It is claimed that it was here that a guest, on seeing his first araucaria – of which there is an avenue at Pencarrow – was the first to remark that 'It would be a puzzle for a monkey'. The Rounds, an ancient encampment and a Celtic cross are joined by later features such the lake and wishing well; ice- and palm-houses; cockpit by the drive, and the ample kitchen garden Sir Arscott Molesworth-St Aubyn, who died in 199 emulated Sir William's extensive planting of coni rhododendrons and camellias.

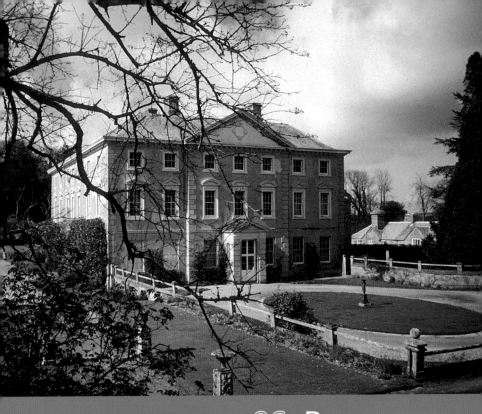

MID-EAST

SX04 53

size	12ha/30a
soil	Alluvial lime-free
altitude	25–15m
aspect	Various
rainfall	114–127cm/45–50in
temperature	Zone D
NC	Grevilleas
	Nursery

The Lodge was acquired by the present owners in 1974. The first task was to build a formal terrace and sunken garden in front of the house, which led into an informal area of lawns. Next was the creation of winding paths through island beds. By the mid-1980s, these were filled with an increasingly wide range of rare and unusual trees, shrubs and other plants. The area beyond was developed into an arboretum, large enough for the specimen trees not to be cramped, and the accessibility of water facilitated the creation of a quite sizeable lake in a field above the house, planted with water lilies. Next the entrance was improved, with a red-brick serpentine pathway through the plantation arriving at the front of the house betwe two waterfalls, cascading down huge rocks and fe ing into a large pond with Koi carp, over which th house is reached by a bridge. The arboretum was extended on one side into a pinetum, where the tr are graded in size eventually to form a semi-circu amphitheatre. The lower side of the arboretum ha been retained as parkland, and a new lake, with black swans and wild ducks, has been formed fro water from mine workings. The 'Slave Garden' wa next to be created – so named from a central featu around which is a circle of herbaceous beds with graded colours, and a collection of 14 magnolias in the surrounding lawn. The most recent addition has been a Japanese Garden, influenced by a visit that country. The over 6,000 plants, many rare if r unique, have all been labelled by Mrs Shirley Clem who has become an expert plantswoman. This bri account vastly understates the great interest and beauty of this garden which, it has been suggeste possesses the finest and most varied collection of plants in Cornwall.

87 Pine Lodge Gardens & Nursery

open	Mar–Oct, daily am, pm
directions	SX12 66, E of Bodmin from A30 roundabout take A38 towards Plymouth, first L to Cardinham and Fletchers Bridge, garden 1.5ml on R
owners	Mark & Claire Woodbine
address	Pinsla Lodge, Cardinham, Bodmin PL30 4AY
enquiries	T: 01208 821339 E: info@pinslagarden. co.uk www.pinslagarden. co.uk

MID-EAST

SX12 66

size	0.6ha/1.5a
soil	Lime-free
altitude	145m
aspect	In a SAGLV
rainfall	114–127cm/45–50in
temperature	Zone F
	Nursery

Situated in the Cardinham Woods, Pinsla in the 17th and 18th centuries had been a deer park attached to the Lanhydrock estate. Today, what is described by the owners as a 'romantic and inspirational' garden surrounds a former lodge of Glynn House, to which they came in 1983. At first, space had to be cut out of the overgrown woodland with an under-growth of laurel. Claire Woodbine – a not inappropriate name in the context! – had formerly worked in the theatrical world, from which she brought an imaginative flair to her designs for the garden. This is almost entirely covered with herbaceous plants and shrub borders, through which wind decorative paths patterned with various slates and cobbles set in con-crete, and forming, with granite boulders, a characteristic feature. The planting provides splashes of contrasting colour, punctuated with dramatic clumps of alliums and yellow rudbeckias. In front, leading from a small rectangular pond, and at the side of the house are mixed beds of low and alpine plants. Sculptures, in painted concrete, coiled metal, withies and bamboo, have been incorporated into the general design. The garden is entered through the nursery, which holds a wide range of plants – over 600 varieties – attractively arranged, many of which, including a good numb of ferns and shade plants, are difficult to find else where, and reflect the style of planting in the gard which is atmospheric and a haven for the plant-lo

88 Pinsla Garden & Nursery

open	Several Suns Mar–May, pm
directions	SX03 50, 2ml SE of St Austell. E on A390 from St Austell, turn R after Asda, signed to Porthpean, take 2nd L after hospital, signed to Lower Porthpean, entrance on L at bottom of hill
owners	Mr & Mrs C. Petherick
address	Porthpean House, Lower Porthpean, St Austell PL26 6AX
enquiries	T: 01726 72888
pronounced	porthPEAN
EH	House: II

MID-EAST

SX03 50

size	1.2ha/3a
soil	Shaly, lime-free (pH6)
altitude	From 45m
aspect	E-sloping
rainfall	102–114cm/40–45in
temperature	Zone D
	Plant sales

The garden at Porthpean, once an inn, was laid o
on a low cliff directly above the beach, by Mauric
Petherick, in the mid-1950s. There is a panorami
view of the sea, particularly from the top of the
garden. At first there was little more than a ragge
line of tamarisks to ward off the salt-laden gales.
These were replaced by a variety of shrubs and t
– bay, elder, ash and pittosporum. In other parts
the garden there are large, well-established beec
chestnuts and Monterey pine, to act as windbreal
Even so, the garden is quite grey with salt after b
gales, and sometimes artificial shelter has to be u
The garden was designed for a collection of cam
lias, of which some 200 were planted during the
five years. Detailed records of the varieties plante
were kept in a card index. A special charm of this
garden is the natural carpet of primroses, which a
generally in flower at the same time as the came

89 Porthpean House Gardens

open	Easter Sun–following Thu; mid-May–early Oct, Sun–Thu, pm
directions	SW91 75, on edge of Padstow, brown signs from ring road (A389)
owners	Mr & Mrs Peter Prideaux-Brune
address	Prideaux Place, Padstow PL28 8RP
enquiries	T: 01841 532411 F: 01841 532945 E: office@prideaux place.co.uk www.prideauxplace.co.uk
pronounced	PRIDoh
EH	House: I; numerous outdoor features II* or II

MID-EAST

SW91 75

EH	Gardens: II
size	c.2ha/5a + deer park c.2ha/5a, in estate 16ha/40a
soil	Lime-free
altitude	55–45m
aspect	E-sloping, in an AONB
rainfall	76–89cm/30–35in
temperature	Zone D

Nicholas Prideaux purchased the fee-simple of P stow at the dissolution of the Priory, thus enablir his descendant to build a 'stately house' there in 1592. Edmund Prideaux, who inherited in 1728, made many alterations, redesigning the garden after a visit to Italy in 1739–40. His keen interest architecture and garden design is evident in a se of sketches made on two tours, in 1716 and 172' chiefly to the houses of his relatives. His depictio of Prideaux shows along the front of the house t existing long terrace, with central steps between lars. To the extreme left is a square building, perl used to house his 'Roman antiquities', an obelisk and the temple. In the foreground, below the terr is an elaborate formal garden. By 1758, when hi: son Humphrey succeeded, fashions were changi Illustrations now show the house as castellated, a the terrace with a central gate-house and embat-tled with cannon. The obelisk had disappeared, b not the temple. The whole foreground had becon a deer park, with a walled garden to the left. This is one of only three deer parks in Cornwall to hav survived to the present day, bearing a legend tha the deer were to die out, so too would the family. When the Revd Charles Pri-deaux-Brune (the 'Brune' was added in response to the will of his maternal uncle) became the owner in 1793, further extensions and alterations were made. The dairy was adorned as a grotto, another being incorporated into the terrace. He continued his rockwork at the stable-yard water trough. The shell house, and the Victorian sunken garden, now restored, and formerly with a handsome conservatory on the end platform, date from 1878 and were designed by Charles Glynn Prideaux-Brune.

90 Prideaux Place

The Ranch House and its busy pottery studio are surrounded by a variety of garden rooms, carefully screened, so that one surprise follows another. An area of lawn with red and pink hydrangeas leads through to the long main lawn. A full-length border contains a colourful mixture of shrubs and herbaceous plants. Opposite, a substantial sheltering hedge curves gently inwards, shielding the far end, so that the roomy, wooden summerhouse comes as a sudden revelation. This hedge appears to be the garden boundary, but little pathways lead through to a perimeter walk with long views across neighbouring farmland. Towards the house, a swing hangs from a mature eucalyptus tree, and nearby a Kiftsgate rose scrambles 11m (35 ft) into the surrounding trees to produce its cloud of white flowers. The terrace, fringed with more hydrangeas, is planted with pink and white, scented roses. The colour theme is continued in the nearby rose garden where the shades of the roses are echoed in the planting of anemones, dahlias a peonies. Fencing of blue posts linked by ornamental ropework contributes to the colour palette, and also adds structure. An orchard enclosure contains a variety of fruit trees, heavily laden in late summm A separate kitchen garden produces a wide variet of crops, thanks to the plentiful supply of rainwate ingeniously collected and transported from the roo of the house. A particular character is given to the garden by the rare breeds of hens, and by the priz winning cockerel whose distant voice evokes a tru country atmosphere.

91 The Ranch House

MID-EAST

SX11 51

The house is converted from the stables and coach house to the large, Italianate villa at Point Neptu. built by the second William Rashleigh (1817–71). From 1942 to 1943, Readymoney was the reside of Daphne du Maurier, where she wrote *Hungry Hill*, before moving to **Menabilly** (126), the mode for 'Manderley' in her novel *Rebecca*. Unlike mos stables, the building had an attractive front, now part covered with the double 'Vyvyan Pennell', 'J manii' and 'Polish Spirit', growing through the ro 'May Queen'; a Passion flower, and a 'japonica'; a along the side, an 'Albertine' rose. The front gard in summer glows with pink hydrangeas, but it is valley to the rear that contains the greatest treasu A stream runs west of the house, where a bog ga containing arum and 'Day' lilies, candelabra prim las, and ferns, fringed with a carpet of geranium overlying springtime bluebells, leads up to the sl ing sides of the valley, which are closely planted a variety of mixed shrubs. Below, along the strea and valley bottom, are colourful herbaceous beds An arbour is draped with the golden hop, a *Clem orientalis* 'Orange Peel', and an akebia. Nearby is a natural bed of marsh orchids bearing over 50 flowers – a genus that is a speciality of Mr Read, who cultivates the more tender species, with hoyas and other South American plants, in his heated greenhouse. Another speciality is bamboos, of which there are some 25 varieties. It is impossible here to do justice to this fascinating garden, which will be of particular interest to the plant-lover.

92 Readymoney Cove

open	By appointment
directions	SX09 15, 8ml NE of Bodmin. From the centre of St Breward village, go down hill 1ml towards Wenford Bridge. At the first crossroads, after grass triangle with red telephone box, turn L opposite the farm lane. The garden is 800yd on the R, immediately after a dangerous bend
owner	Mrs Paddy Powell
address	Rose Cottage, De Lank, St Breward, Bodmin PL30 4ND
enquiries	T: 01208 850186

MID-EAST

SX09 15 ___

size	0.4ha/1a
soil	Lime-free
aspect	Sloping W from 120m, in a SAGLV
rainfall	102–114cm/40–45in
temperature	Zone E
	Plant sales

Rose Cottage is the first in a line of cottages that nestle on a bend below the level of the road, protected in a hollow. This colourful garden, bright with white and pink poppies, surrounds these dwelling in a characteristically cottagey, though nonetheless refined style. The sections are arranged not so much in compartments, but as they relate to the individual buildings. In front of Rose Cottage the lawn is small to the left a little pond is fed by water cascading from an ornamental fish's mouth. Alongside is a silver border, with both shrubby and herbaceous senecio, perovskia and argyranthemums. This leads up to an urn, which forms the focal point of this garden, where steps lead to a gate bordered with a *Rhododendron yakushimanum*, azaleas, camellias, and a *Magnolia stellata*. From this point the drive, along which visitors enter, dips down to The Hollow. At end is a charming, detached 17th-century house mullioned windows, against which grows a *Magnolia grandiflora*. The side, where a pergola is covered with wisteria, faces a triangular lawn. Opposite is the 'Arbour' garden, where the sunny seat looks over the countryside, and the shady seat is flanked by meconopsis. The path extends down this side through the two long herbaceous borders, with apricot and white foxgloves and a bed of hostas. A *Magnolia wilsonii* has been strategically planted on a bank, where one can look up into the hanging cups of the flowers. On the other side of the lawn, the stream has been shaped into a cascade, so that after rain the sound of babbling water is heard from afar. Rose Cottage has been open locally for over ten years, but is now, by request, open to a wider public.

93 Rose Cottage

open	Jan, Feb, Sats, Suns, pm
directions	SW91 48, 1ml from Grampound off A390; lane entrance is 100yd W of Grampound Road crossroads and 0.5ml E of Trewithen roundabout
owners	Mr & Mrs K.A. O'Connor
address	Tregoose, Grampound, Truro TR2 4DB
enquiries	T: 01726 882460
pronounced	treGOOSE

P
☕

MID-EAST

SW91 48

size	Small to medium
soil	Lime-free
altitude	75m
aspect	S-facing
rainfall	102–114cm/40–45in
temperature	Zone D
	Plant sales

The sight of Tregoose, surrounded by trees, lying below to the left of the road to Grampound just after the entrance to Trewithen, has always been intriguing, and so its opening has satisfied any curiosity about the nature of the garden within. The house was built in 1840 for the agent of the nearby Trewithen estate, although it has since been extended. The grounds were originally laid out in lawns with a shelter belt of mature trees, and have been developed since about 1980 by Mrs O'Connor, who is herself a trained horticulturist. The garden has been planted for all-year interest. At the entrance, one is at once struck by a free-standing *Magnolia grandiflora* 'Goliath', and by fine bushes of camellias, such as 'Freedom Bell' – one of the few red *williamsii*. Another *Magnolia grandiflora* – 'Exmouth' – adorns the front of the house, joined by the climbing, hydrangea-like pilostegia. In the conservatory adjoining the house, the glorious flowers of *Camellia rosiflora* 'Royalty' benefit from the shelter, as do brugmansia and ipomoea. Everywhere the plants are varieties of distinction or rarity – a *Magnolia mollicomata* is a seedling from **Caerhays** (71); a pieris near the house is the recent 'Dorothy Wyckoff' variety; while among the daffodils, the hybrid 'Green Howard' is rarely seen elsewhere. There is also an expanding collection of snowdrops. One of the m[ost] recent features is the creation of a potager behind the house. The walled garden is quartered into fo[ur] herbaceous beds – one overtopped by an *Acacia b[ai]leyana* 'Purpurea' – which are colourful in summe[r]

open	Mid-Mar–mid-Jun, Wed–Sun, excl Easter Sun, + bank holiday Mons, am, pm; also Wed only, mid-Jun–Aug, pm
directions	SX05 53, entrance on A390 opposite Britannia Inn
owner	Mr T.C. Hudson
address	Tregrehan, Par, St Austell PL24 2SJ
enquiries	T: 01726 812438 F: 01726 814389 www.tregrehan.org
pronounced	treGRAIN
EH	House: II

MID-EAST

SX05 53

EH	Garden: II*
size	8ha/20a
soil	Lime-free
altitude	65–15m, house at 55m
aspect	S-facing slope
rainfall	114–127cm/45–50in
temperature	Zone D
	Plant sales

Formerly in the possession of the Brodrugans and Edgcumbes, since 1565 Tregrehan has been occupied by the Carlyon family, who extensively planted the parkland during the 18th century. In 1840 the house was remodelled by the Cornish architect George Wightwick for Edward Carlyon, who also invited the up-and-coming Nesfield to design a parterre to the south of the enlarged house, with a new Entrance Court for the West Front. Nesfield's original plan, dated 1843, is still preserved at Tregrehan. His labour-intensive parterres, in the style known as 'broderie', composed of coloured gravel and grass, have now gone, but the terrace in front of the house, with its stone balustrading, urns, and statues of the Four Seasons still survive. The circular pool with its 'charming dolphin fountain', which forms a central feature in the large, walled kitchen garden, created at the same time, is also believed to have been designed by Nesfield. This garden, now restyled, also contains a fine range of greenhouses. Edgar Thurston, in 1930, had written that 'The fine Pinetum is a special feature of the grounds, which contain one of the choicest collections of rare trees and shrubs in the County', reflecting the opinion of W.J. Bean, who had visited Tregrehan in 1916, and it has always been for its collection of trees that Tregrehan has been celebrated. Many of these – now of magnificent size – still survive, among them two avenues of stately yews. Today, there have been added many new specimens from the Southern hemisphere, reflecting the family's interest in New Zealand. In recent years, the garden has also become famous for the camellia hybrids raised by the late Miss Gillian Carlyon.

95 Tregrehan

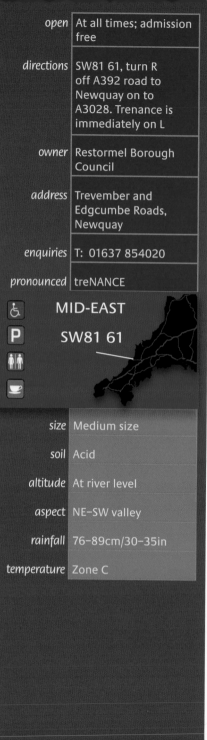

open	At all times; admission free
directions	SW81 61, turn R off A392 road to Newquay on to A3028. Trenance is immediately on L
owner	Restormel Borough Council
address	Trevember and Edgcumbe Roads, Newquay
enquiries	T: 01637 854020
pronounced	treNANCE

MID-EAST

SW81 61

size	Medium size
soil	Acid
altitude	At river level
aspect	NE–SW valley
rainfall	76–89cm/30–35in
temperature	Zone C

With the growth of the holiday industry in Newquay, the upper part of the Trenance Valley at the rear of the town was laid out in 1906 as a public garden, and the narrow track widened for vehicles. The sunny, sheltered nature of this valley was considered a pleasant contrast for visitors to the more bracing air of the sands and cliffs. The gardens had the advantage – especially in an area that is predominantly alkaline – of having on the slopes a thin, acid soil in which camellias, rhododendrons and heathers could be grown. In 1933 the gardens were extended to provide a large boating lake, a quarter of a mile (0.4km) lc by damming the stream flowing into the Gannel, around which were planted flower gardens. These gardens have been extended into a large leisure a occupying over 16 acres (6.5ha). Today, the slopes have become the site of the Lakeside Café, and m of the area surrounding the lake has been laid to lawn. The islands, however, are furnished with tre and on the largest are three 'willow men' by Seren de la Hey, looking out into the distant countryside. the northern end of the lake, on the site of a form nursery, a fine rose garden was planted in 1993, with a pergola, and metal obelisks in the centre of the beds for climbers. This has the great benefit of a permanent plan, by which all the varieties can b easily identified. The formal flower gardens are in separate area across a side road. Here there is opp tunity to relax in a peaceful atmosphere, and to en the colourful bedding schemes.

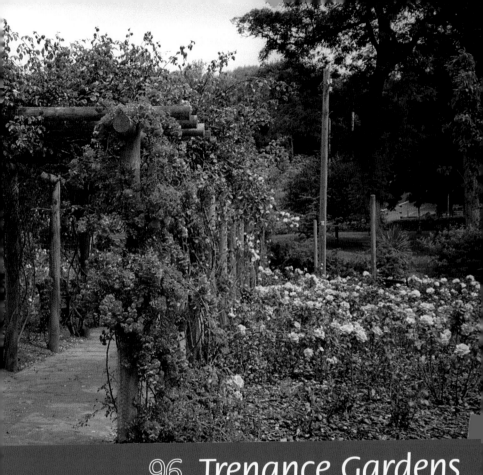

96 Trenance Gardens

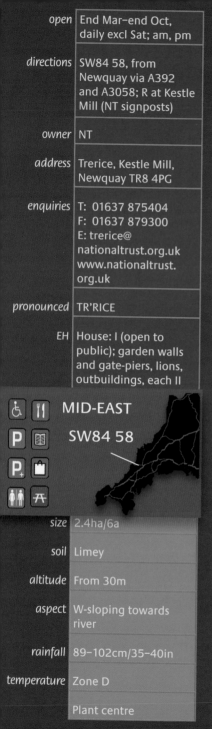

open	End Mar–end Oct, daily excl Sat; am, pm
directions	SW84 58, from Newquay via A392 and A3058; R at Kestle Mill (NT signposts)
owner	NT
address	Trerice, Kestle Mill, Newquay TR8 4PG
enquiries	T: 01637 875404 F: 01637 879300 E: trerice@ nationaltrust.org.uk www.nationaltrust. org.uk
pronounced	TR'RICE
EH	House: I (open to public); garden walls and gate-piers, lions, outbuildings, each II

MID-EAST

SW84 58

size	2.4ha/6a
soil	Limey
altitude	From 30m
aspect	W-sloping towards river
rainfall	89–102cm/35–40in
temperature	Zone D
	Plant centre

A former Domesday manor, Trerice came by marriage to the Arundells in about 1330. The Elizabethan house was built for Sir John Arundell in about 1570, and was described by Michael Trinick of the National Trust as half-hidden

> by elms, its curving grey gables command no distant view, for this is a close country, and Elizabethan builders cared more for sheltered places, and the presence of pure spring water, than for a wide prospect.

By default of male issue, the estate eventually passed from the Arundells to the Aclands.

Gilbert, in his *Historical Survey* of 1822, found 'little appearance of its once fruitful gardens, raised terrace, and expansive lakes.' The gardens as they are now seen have been laid out since the National Trust came into possession of the house in 1953, but with due regard for the style and antiquity of the site. The forecourt, once probably cobbled, was turfed and planted with borders in 1969; the present garden walls probably date from no earlier than the beginning of the 19th century. From this forecourt, steps lead up north to the bowling green, also a 19th-century addition with level terraces above, all of a type described by Graham Stuart Thomas as 'nearly unique in Cornwall'. To the south, old illustrations show a 'Dutch Garden', but all signs of this have vanished and in 1972 this area was planted with herbaceous borders, and an orchard with a collection of old apples, arranged in a *quincunx* pattern, where the trees are in line from whichever angle they are viewed. The Arundell lions, originally from Kenegie near Penzance, were rescued by the National Trust from Lifton in Devon, and brought here for safety. There is an interesting museum of lawnmowers.

open	Groups by appointment only
directions	SW85 58, A3058 from Newquay 1ml on R past Kestle Mill
contact	Mr John Harris c/o Trevarthian Cottage, Kestle Mill, Newquay TR8 4PQ
address	Tresillian House, Summercourt, Newquay TR8 4PS
enquiries	T: 07979 527840 or 01637 877447 E: rjohn.harris@ btinternet.com www.moongardening .fsnet.co.uk
pronounced	treSILLian
EH	House: II

MID-EAST

SW85 58

size	12ha/30a, in 80ha/ 200a estate
soil	Alkaline
altitude	70–55m
aspect	W-sloping
rainfall	89–102cm/35–40in
temperature	Zone D

The core of the present house at Tresillian was built in 1792, and remodelled in 1820, but when Capt. Leonard Bennet inherited his uncle's estate in 1928, he found the house neglected, and the grounds overgrown. He proceeded at once to cut down trees to open up the pond to view; built a greenhouse; erected a pergola, and planted flowering shrubs. In 1947, after the Second World War, the estate was sold, and in the 1970s became the residence of the owner of the home farm (which was run as a theme park, 'Dairyland'), who further developed the grounds. From the late 1980s the walled garden, which dates from the 18th century, was laid out in Victorian style, by the knowledgeable head gardener, John Harris, with old varieties, and plants formerly used as organic remedies against pests and diseases. In 1993, he began a reference collection of 100 varieties of apples – 78 of Cornish origin – interspersed with medlars and quinces, as part of a plan to create at Tresillian an authentic representation of historic gardening practices in the county. Harris's expertise and advice were to prove invaluable during the restoration of **Heligan** (81).

Tresillian estate was sold to the present owner in 2000. The two Victorian greenhouses have been rebuilt under the guidance of John Harris. The Elizabethan barns a outbuildings are undergoing major restoration w which will include a large conference hall. The ga dens are to be further extended, to include the cre tion of two large camellia shrubberies. The garde Tresillian is entirely organic, and lunar-orientated

98 Tresillian House Garden

Bude and North-East Cornwall

Gardens in the extreme north of the county, open to the sea and the ravages of the north and north-west winds, are thin on the ground. For example, along this strip, west of the A39 from Port Isaac to the county border at Morwenstowe, only six places received mention in the historic records as possessing any sort of garden. Moreover, except for Bude, which is not of any great antiquity, and perhaps Camelford, there is no town of substance in the whole of this region north of Wade-bridge. This is not to say that there were no settlements or old manor houses in this area; indeed, they were probably just as frequent as in other localities, but they were not in situations that encouraged their development into mansions with parks, or were such as would lead to the creation of new estates during the years of prosperity.

(See gardens 101, 105, 110, 116, 120.)

Launceston

The dearth of gardens in the previous section, along the exposed western side of Bodmin Moor, was a consequence of the isolation of the region from the mainstream of traffic, and the harsher geographical factors. Here on the eastern side of the Moor, the gardens have been influenced more by the configuration of the rivers that span the area, than by their proximity to Launceston, ancient and important though that town may have been. The Tamar, along the whole of its length, forms the border of Cornwall with Devon, but it has been its tributaries, such as the Ottery, the Inney, and especially the Lynher, which have influenced the distribution of gardens. The Ottery, for instance, flows through **Werrington** (131) to form a distinctive feature and feed a lake, until eventually joining the Tamar close to the borders of the Park. **Penheale Manor** (114), with two lakes, also benefits from streams that run into the Ottery. Launceston itself stands a little west of the river on another smaller tributary, the Kensey. The greatest of the tributaries – the Lynher – which, by the time it meets the Tamar at its mouth, will have swollen sufficiently to have become its rival, begins as a trickle flowing down from the Moors, and rushes as a cataract into the grounds of **Trebartha** (117) to feed the swan pond. More peaceably, a few miles south at Berriow Bridge, the village gardens have sometimes opened to the public.

(See gardens 107, 114, 117, 118.)

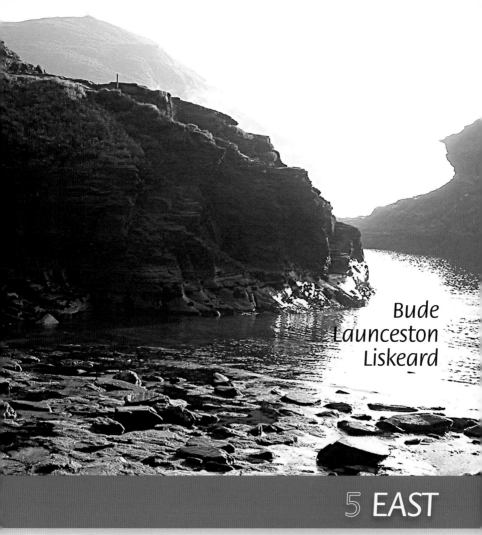

Bude
Launceston
Liskeard

5 EAST

eard and South-East Cornwall
final section covers a broad area of
rior, coastal and riverside landscape,
ected by river valleys that make com-
nications roundabout and difficult.
n towns as there are tend to serve
s confined within natural boundaries,
n with its own characteristics and
d justification. To the west, Liskeard,
e with a castle and two deer parks,
at the head of the long valley of the
Looe river, which opens into the sea
ost due south. **Moyclare** (113), on its
kirts, has an interesting contemporary
len. To the east of Looe is St Ger-

man's, where the River Lynher opens out
into the Tamar to form the twin estuary of
the Hamoaze. Here is **Port Eliot** (128), one
of the two gardens in mainland Cornwall
with an English Heritage Grade I for
national significance. East of St German's,
towards Saltash and Torpoint, the great
natural beauty of the landscape has given
birth to many parks and gardens, chief
among them **Mount Edgcumbe** (112), the
other of the Grade I gardens, and along
the Tamar **Antony** (99), **Ince Castle** (108),
Pentillie (127), and **Cotehele** (102).

(See gardens 99, 100, 102, 103, 104,
106, 108, 109, 111, 112, 113, 115, 116.)

open	Apr–Oct, Tue–Thu, + bank holiday Mons + Sun Jun, Jul, Aug, pm
directions	SX41 56, entrance off A374 on outskirts of Torpoint
owner	NT
address	Antony House, Torpoint PL11 2QA
enquiries	T/F: 01752 812364 E: antony@ nationaltrust.org.uk www.national trust.org.uk
EH	House: I (open to public); dovecote II*; kitchen garden walls, claire-voie, bath house, dovecote (remains), II

EAST

SX41 56

EH	Gardens: II*
size	10ha/25a
soil	Lime-free, medium loam on shale
altitude	60m–sea; house 25m
aspect	NW-sloping to sea, in an AONB and SAGLV
rainfall	89–102cm/35–40cm
temperature	Zone D
NC	600 Day Lilies (*Hemerocallis*)

The Domesday manor had a long history before the arrival there of the Carews in the late 15th century, of whom the most celebrated was Richard Carew, author of the first *Survey of Cornwall* (1602). The present house was built between 1711 and 1721 on a new site. A sketch of the garden front by Edmund Prideaux in 1727 shows the dovecote, which still survives, and an elaborate, formal walled garden with radiating avenues beyond. This formality was swept away on the recommendation of Humphry Repton, who prepared a 'Red Book' in 1792. In the 19th century, the *porte-cochère* was added to the front of the house, and vistas were cut through the perimeter belt of trees to Shillingham on the other side of the river. The first yew walks were begun, and were extended in the 20th century. It was at this time that the garden's reputation began to grow. The family were encouraged and assisted in the development of the garden by J.C. Williams of **Caerhays** (71) and Lionel de Rothschild of Exbury, which led to the introduction of a great variety of azaleas, rhododendrons and magnolias. An enclosed Summer Garden was begun in 1983 by Lady Mary Carew Pole, who also designed the Knot Garden. A National Colle of 600 Day Lilies (*Hemerocallis*) was assembled b the present Sir Richard's mother, Lady Cynthia C Pole. Antony House was donated to the National Trust in 1961, and the Trust has continued to develop the garden. A number of modern sculptures have been sensitively introduced, including *Hypezlone* by Simon Cook (p. 223). The management of the original woodland at Antony has been separated (see 100).

99 Antony House & Garden

Mar–Oct, daily excl Mon and Fri, but open bank holidays, am, pm	
SX41 56, entrance off A374 on outskirts of Torpoint	
Carew Pole Garden Trust	
Antony House, Torpoint PL11 2QA	
T/F: 01752 812364 E: pcressy@savills.com	

EAST

X41 56

40ha/100a woodland
Lime-free, medium loam on shale
From 60m to river level
NW-sloping, in a SAGLV and AONB
89–102cm/35–40in
Zone D
Camellia japonica

The extensive woodland gardens were not taken over with **Antony House** and formal garden (99) by the National Trust, but have remained separately managed by the Carew Pole Garden Trust. Since 1984, Sir Richard Carew Pole, who was elected President of the RHS in 2001, has been involved in its ongoing development. The woodlands may be visited on their own, or there are various routes from the garden, along wandering pathways designed to reveal the many beauties and vistas from the woods. In spring the glades are carpeted with primroses, bluebells, campions, and the beautiful but pungent wild garlic. Spring is also the season first for camellias – of which Antony has a National Collection of *Camellia japonica* – and the magnolias, planted in the 1950s, for which Sir Richard has a special enthusiasm. There is a named collection of 103 magnolias at Antony. The northern edge of the Woodland Gardens is marked by Jupiter Point, so named from the figurehead of a ship once placed there, but now decayed. In its place is a large granite stone in memory of Sir John and Lady Cynthia Carew Pole, who were responsible for so much of the planting over the last 50 years, which bears an apt inscription from *Omar Khayam* – 'And still a garden by the water blows'. There are rhododendrons to follow, and acers, which are at their best later in the year; while the many varieties of conifer maintain their beauty and interest throughout the year. There are over 6,000 plants in the Antony list, and these woodla will provide a feast for the tree-lover.

100 Antony Woodland Garden

open	Three days for NGS, one day for Cornwall Wildlife Trust. Any Sat or Sun if fine, am, pm. Ring to check
directions	SS19 00, from A39 take Widemouth/Bude coastal route. L at Widemouth Manor Hotel for 0.5ml. L up lane
owners	Tim & Sandy Dingle
address	The Barn House, Poundstock, Bude EX23 0DG
enquiries	T: 01288 361356

EAST

SS19 00

size	0.2ha/0.5a garden in 4ha/10a
soil	Neutral to acid
altitude	75m
aspect	SW, in an AONB
rainfall	89cm/35in
temperature	Zone E
	Plant sales

Barn House, not far from the north Cornish coast and swept by strong, salt-laden winter winds, demonstrates just what can be achieved with imagination and careful planning. When Sandy and Tim Dingle took over the property they started with a blank canvas, apart from a few mature apple trees. They have created a garden of wide lawns, fringed by enclaves carefully protected by a variety of sheltering planting, including escallonia, griselinia and phormiums. Wide borders of shrubs and herbaceous plants are designed to give colour throughout the year. One especially windy bed has been given prairie planting, and glows with the yellows and purples of *Verbena bonariensis*, marigolds, oenotheras and margueriites,

enriched by agaves and cacti from the greenhous The apple trees now form a discrete orchard area underplanted with more tender specimens includ ing a delicate acer. An adjoining area, tucked intc the contour of the land and sheltered by shrub rc contains the pond, with large-leaved water-lilies a cyperus, fringed by deep pink dierama. The edge gently pebbled slope, designed to be wildlife frie Close by, a good vantage point is the Captain's Se formed from an old wooden hatch cover. A path- way leads out of the formal garden down to a wa through a wooded valley, filled with bluebells in early summer and a rich haven for wildlife. On q mornings, red and roe deer can be spotted passin through; foxes and badgers are frequent visitors, the area is particularly rich in butterflies.

101 Barn House

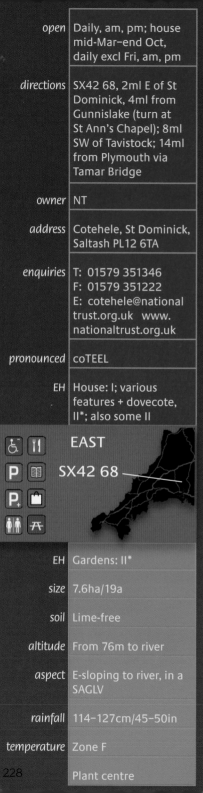

open	Daily, am, pm; house mid-Mar–end Oct, daily excl Fri, am, pm
directions	SX42 68, 2ml E of St Dominick, 4ml from Gunnislake (turn at St Ann's Chapel); 8ml SW of Tavistock; 14ml from Plymouth via Tamar Bridge
owner	NT
address	Cotehele, St Dominick, Saltash PL12 6TA
enquiries	T: 01579 351346 F: 01579 351222 E: cotehele@national trust.org.uk www. nationaltrust.org.uk
pronounced	coTEEL
EH	House: I; various features + dovecote, II*; also some II

EAST

SX42 68

EH	Gardens: II*
size	7.6ha/19a
soil	Lime-free
altitude	From 76m to river
aspect	E-sloping to river, in a SAGLV
rainfall	114–127cm/45–50in
temperature	Zone F
	Plant centre

Pevsner judged Cotehele to be 'the most extensiv and important Tudor house of Cornwall'. The old house, of which remnants remain in the lower wa was remodelled for Sir Richard Edgcumbe and hi son Piers in the late 15th century. Norden's map c. 1690 shows two deer parks, and the medieval dovecote still survives. The oak and chestnut tree which are of great antiquity, although scarcely th 1,000 years suggested by a writer in 1842, regula caused 'astonishment', and in 1799 the yews wer reckoned to be 'some of the largest ... in England The Edgcumbes transferred to **Mount Edgcumbe** (112) in about 1553, after which Cotehele was no more than an occasional residence. The house wa again remodelled in about 1862, when the terrac were laid out 'in old-fashioned beds and borders filled with hardy flowers'. In more recent years, si Cotehele has been in the care of the National Tru the gardens have been greatly developed. Below terraces, and across the road in the upper valley den, are the dovecote, a 19th-century summerhouse, and a small lake, which was probably the medieval stew-pond. Below, the lower valley becomes densely wooded, with clearings and pools with shrubs and water-loving plants. In the upper garden, to the north-east of the house, there is a square pond with lilies, and nearby an orchard. It was noted in 1893 that: 'This place' was 'the centre of very extensive fruit gardens, hundreds of acres being devoted to Cherries, Strawberries, Raspberries, Plums, &c.', although not all, of course, on the Cotehele estate itself.

open	Alternate years under 'Menheniot Gardens': see NGS yellow book; or by appointment
directions	SX29 62, 4ml along A38 from Liskeard to Plymouth, take Menheniot turning NE. After 1ml turn sharp R at Cricket Club sign; house at end of track
owners	Julian & Valerie Sturdy
address	East Down Barn, Menheniot PL14 3QU
enquiries	See NGS annual yellow book, or www.ngs.org.uk

P

EAST

SX29 62

size	0.3ha/0.75a
soil	Lime-free
altitude	100–85m
aspect	E-sloping
rainfall	114–127cm/45–50in
temperature	Zone F
	Plant sales

The garden at East Down Barn, along a lane on the outskirts of Menheniot, has been created since 1992 on a slope dropping sharply down to a stream in a narrow valley. On the level by the house is a bank, and a large circular bed by the front entrance crowded with alpines and the smaller herbaceous plants, such as campanula, geraniums, and the daisy-flowered *Erigeron* 'Profusion'. On the bank, the curious cerinthe with grey leaves and striking blue flowers catches the eye. The steep, almost precipitate slope has been terraced and planted with mixed borders of cistus, lavenders, poppies and foxgloves. Several large specimens of the 'Beauty Bush' *Kolkwitzia amabilis* stand out when flowering profusely. Leading on to a narrow lawn is a rustic pergola, covered by clematis, roses and the golden hop, alongside which is a novel gravel bed with ornamental grasses and other spiky plants. In a corner grows the handsome tiered *Cornus contoversa*, sometimes called the 'Wedding Cake Tree'. The lawn runs down to a boggy area by the stream, over which is a wooden bridge. Here the natural planting includes as well as wild grasses and ferns, the candelabra primulas. Valerie Sturdy was a finalist in the BBC television programme 'Gardener of the Year 2000', and winner of the Garden Knowledge Challenge Section. This garden display an interesting range and combination of plants, a the very difficult site has been managed in an exp way, which will serve as an ideal model for those who face similar problems.

103 East Down Barn

open	Apr–Jul, by appointment
directions	SX18 73, from Jamaica Inn off A30 at Bolventor, take road south to Colliford Lake and St Neot, 2.5ml to Higher Gillhouse
owners	John & Iris Stanton
address	Higher Gillhouse, St Neot, Liskeard PL14 6PY
enquiries	T: 01579 320789 E: irisstanton@ hotmail.com

EAST
SX18 73

size	1.2ha/3a
soil	Acid (peat)
altitude	290m
aspect	In an AONB
rainfall	178–190cm/70–75in
temperature	Zone F
	Plant sales

At 290m (950ft) altitude, Gillhouse is the highest den in Cornwall, but although it is set in moorlan is not moorland in character. Mr Stanton, who ca here with his wife in 1988, had worked as head g dener in several places, including Haseley Court Oxfordshire – a far cry from Bodmin Moor. An ea attempt to grow trees was unsuccessful, but now, chiefly with herbaceous and lower-growing plan sheltered by hedges, it has proved possible to cre a flourishing and colourful garden. The position, sloping gently down to the shores of Colliford La opens up several vistas across to the tors of the h moor. Upon entering, the garden radiates in three directions. In the centre, a granite path leads up t the house, alongside which a colourful herbaceou border nestles against the hedge. From the top of this hedge can be viewed a surprising V-shaped terre, filled principally with red-leafed begonias, contrasting edging. On the right, a moorland stre that runs underground has emerged to channel it into a small pool before again draining away. At t top of the path, nearer the house, an enclosed are suitable for sitting and relaxing is ablaze with col – crocosmias; the 'Bishop of Llandaff' dahlia; pur thalictrum, and other bright plants. The garden continues to the south with island beds, a small pool, and a productive vegetable garden with tunnels, to complete an unexpected display in a spectacular setting.

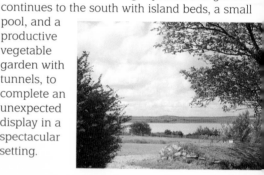

open	One weekend in Jul for NGS. Autumn Exhibition for 2 days; groups by appointment, pm
directions	SW09 90, from Camelford N on B3266 to outskirts of Boscastle. Park as directed and proceed on foot
owners	Carole Vincent
address	Half Acre, Boscastle PL35 0BJ
enquiries	T: 01840 250263

EAST
SW09 90

size	0.5ha/1a
soil	Slightly alkaline
altitude	100m
aspect	N, in an AONB
rainfall	102–114cm/40–45in
temperature	Zone E
	Plant sales

'It is possible to have a colourful environment not only in the plants but in the hard landscape.' This is the inspiration of sculptor Carole Vincent, demonstrated in the medal-winning Blue Circle Cement garden she transferred from Half Acre to the RHS Chelsea Flower Show in 2001. There are two ponds: oval at ground level, and a higher, circular one, together with spiral steps and coloured perimeter walls. Shrubs and potted plants surround the area, which provides the context for carefully sited sculptures. Concrete sculptures in both natural and spectrum colours are strategically located throughout her entire garden in small spaces, commanding a view, or glimpsed from a distance. Carole's garden has always been a designed space. She realized her original dream of 'a cottage by the sea with roses round the door' in the period after her arrival at Half Acre in 1961. Her written plans for a cottage garden, responding to the curves of the local coastline, still exist. She created large sweeping lawns and flowerbeds, establishing a variety of levels and creating small spaces filled with plants carefully selected for a coastal site. Parts of this original garden survive, but the space is constantly reinterpreted to accommodate new inspirations. Extra land acquired more recently offers many possibilities. At present it is treated as natural woodland, and is the site of Carole's 'dead hedge'. This construction of material too big to compost is an excellent protection from the strong winds, and provides a good wildlife habitat.

open	Two Suns in Aug, pm; groups of 10+ by appointment
directions	SX43 62, turn off A388 between St Mellion and Hatt signed to Cargreen; garden next to chapel, where facilities are located
owners	Mr & Mrs B.J. Richards
address	Highcroft Gardens, Cargreen, Saltash PL12 6PA
enquiries	T: 01752 842219 F: 01752 848769 E: highcroftnursery@ btconnect.com

EAST

SX43 62

size	1.2ha/3a
soil	Neutral, sandy loam
aspect	N-sloping from 45m, in an AONB and SAGLV
rainfall	114–127cm/45–50in
temperature	Zone E
	Plant sales

This garden, created since the early 1980s, was described as a 'relaxation' from the daily tasks in a market garden (not open to the public) with extensive greenhouses, specializing in some 28 varieties of alstromerias. The entrance drive arrives at the front of the house, where a new rock garden has replaced some overgrown shrubs. Hidden to the rear is a 'Japanese' garden with a summerhouse, where a serpentine rill runs through the paving to a central pump. Since the flow of water became problematic, the rill has been filled with intense blue glass chippings, the colour being taken up by the surrounding blue pots filled with acers. The front lawn, with two large island beds with herbaceous plants – spurge, zebra grass and sedum – is backed by evergreen shrubs, camellias, and the variegated pieris, to provide all-year colour. Gravel paths lead out from this home garden, threading their way through wide beds of mixed plantings of shrubs and herbaceous plants designed to produce spectacular combinations of colour – a 'hot bed' of reds and oranges; the *Cotinus* 'Royal Purple' against *Lonicera* 'Baggesen's Gold'; silver perovskia against *Cornus alba* 'Aurea'. A long gravel path, with arches of clematis, runs the whole length of this garden, with a roofed 'lych' gate leading out into the lower garden, through which, on looking back, the chapel can be seen in the distance. The lower slopes, where path is bordered with hydrangeas, are planted wi specimen trees and more herbaceous borders. Pr planting, which occupies an area of 0.3a (0.13ha contains over 2,500 grass and herbaceous plants In late summer, the path winding through this ar is a riot of colour. This sensational garden has be featured in magazines, and is one of the few Cor gardens to be at its height in the summer.

106 Highcroft Gardens

open	One Sun each in May, Jun, pm, for NGS
directions	SX30 85, take Egloskerry turn out of St Stephens; first L to Truscott
owner	John Mann
address	Higher Truscott, St Stephens, Launceston PL15 8LA
enquiries	T: 01566 772755

EAST

SX30 85 _____

size	0.4ha/1a
soil	Neutral
altitude	170m
aspect	S-sloping
rainfall	102–114cm/40–45in
temperature	Zone G
	Plant sales

This garden, as its name suggests, is set at a high altitude, sloping gently to the south, but exposed to damaging winds from the east. Higher Truscott is an old long-house with later farm buildings. The garden was originally created in 1966 in the yard this old farm, as an adjunct to be viewed from the house. Nearby, there has been an attempt to grow alpines in gravel, rock beds and troughs, which have not always been successful in this climate, but a small greenhouse in a courtyard serves as an alpine house. Across a lawn, at the farther end of the house garden, trees and shrubs have been planted – camellias, rhododendrons and magnolias, with underplantings of fritillarias and hellebores. The soil here is shallow and stony, so that plants suffer from both wet and dry spells. In 1980 a second garden was begun across the road in a field, which, although if anything more exposed, has a fine view beyond Launceston Castle all the way to Dartmoor. This has provided an opportunity to develop island beds with herbaceous plants, to create colour in the summer. Beyond the summer garden is the kitchen garden, which by way of contrast is of a formal design, with beds edged with box or herbs, in which the vegetables and fruit are neatly arranged. John Mann is a keen and knowledgeable gardener, a member of the Hardy Plant Society, and President of the Cornwall Garden Society.

107 Higher Truscott

open	One Sun each in Mar–May and Jul, pm
directions	SX40 56, turn off A38 to Trematon; signed thereafter
owners	Lord & Lady Boyd
address	Ince Castle, Trematon, Saltash PL12 4QZ
enquiries	T: 01752 842672 F: 01752 847134 boydince@aol.com
pronounced	INS as in 'instant'
EH	House: I

EAST

SX40 56

size	2ha/5a
soil	Lime-free shale
altitude	From 25m
aspect	SW- and SE-sloping to river, in a SAGLV
rainfall	102–114cm/40–45in
temperature	Zone D

Although an ancient site, the remarkable series o gardens at Ince have been created only since 196 by the late Viscountess Boyd and her husband. O entering from the car-park, the 'Summer Garden' aglow with fiery herbaceous plants leads on to th swimming pool, with stone obelisks at each corner, and a panoramic view across the Lynher rive Proceeding towards the south front of the house, we arrive at three gardens, the lower being the li pond, which has at each end a lead *putto* riding a snail. At the western end, the interior of the 'Sh House' glistens with a mosaic of exotic shells. Fro the lily pond, the house is seen beyond the forma garden, quartered by paths with obelisks echoing the theme at the swimming pool, the four beds fi with herbaceous plants. Beyond is a wide paved with a central tank and fountain. Off to the right, more recent 'Castle Garden' is also quartered, wit lawns of camomile, thyme and pink and white th while nearby, from the 'Mound', is a distant view of Plymouth. To the left of the paved area, a long path leads towards the kitchen garden, with the tennis court on the right. There are two paths richly planted on each side with deep mixed borders. North of the house is the woodland garden, with a wide variety of trees, where an oval glade opens on to a water garden. There is a dovecote, among other features, many of which were brought from the courtyard of Lady Boyd's father's house in St James's Square, London. Ince is among the premier contemporary gardens in Cornwall.

open	End Feb–end Sep, Sun–Fri, am, pm
directions	SX31 69, 1ml off A390. Turn N at Butchers Arms, St Ive; follow brown tourist signs
owners	Mr & Mrs K.R. Willcock
address	Ken-Caro, Bicton, nr Liskeard PL14 5RF
enquiries	T: 01579 362446
pronounced	KEN CARo as in arrow

EAST

SX31 69

size	2ha/5a
soil	Very acid
altitude	175m
aspect	E-sloping, in an AGLV, AONB, SAGLV
rainfall	114–127cm/45–50in
temperature	Zone F
	Plant sales

Ken-Caro is set high above Bicton Manor and Woods, whose former deer park is reflected in its name. The garden, begun in 1970, was created around a small bungalow, protected from the wind by high hedges. Some 20 years later it began to be extended into the meadow beyond. This was followed by the erection of a more substantial house, dressed with neatly planted bedding. The new garden of four acres (1.6ha) has been designed on rather different lines from the original, but with the same skill in the selection and association of plants by Mrs Willcock and her husband Kenneth, who is well known for his floristry, and writes a regular column in the *Cornish Gardener*. The new garden is more open; laid out in sweeping island beds, arranged to lead the eye out into the distant landscape, and with a summerhouse at a strategic high point. The beds are mixed shrub and herbaceous plantings, wide enough for paths to thread through them for a closer look. Everywhere the care in plant associations is evident – a *Ligularia* 'Yellow Rocket' contrasts with a purple berberis; a *Rubus* 'Gold Vale' enhances the intense blue of a *Ceanothus* 'Concha'. There are various features in the garden: a circular pergola enclosing a small raised pool is clothed with honeysuck and roses; at a higher level, a large pond affords opportunity to grow bog and water plants. There even a small bed devoted to insectivorous plants with nearby a curious natural 'sculpture' made fr driftwood, and another by the pond. Ken-Caro wi interest the plantsman, but cannot fail to delight everyone.

109 Ken-Caro

open	Two Suns each May, Jun, pm
directions	SX05 84, on B3314 from Pendoggett turn L, or from Delabole turn R at Westdowns, signed to Treligga. Turn L after entering hamlet. Long Hay 30yd on L with white gate. Park in farmyard
owners	Bett & Mick Hartley
address	Long Hay, Treligga, Delabole PL33 9EE
enquiries	T: 01840 212506 See NGS yellow book or www.ngs.org.uk

P

EAST

SX05 84

size	0.7ha/1.75a
soil	Lime-free
altitude	130m
aspect	In an AONB
rainfall	89–102cm/35–40in
temperature	Zone E
	Plant sales

On entering the tiny front garden of Long Hay – a small, cottage-style garden set in a remote village near the north coast – the house is seen half-shielded by a shapely juniper. A *Phlomis fructicosa* grows out of the hedge at the gate, and the bed curving around to the rear has a variety of unusual plants, among them an exochorda, which flowers in the spring. To the rear of the house, the mixed herbaceous beds are dense with a variety of colourful plants, topped by delphiniums and lupins. In the midst of these beds is a small pool. Mrs Hartley has added to her more conventional gardening interests a love of succulents, so there are the hardy sempervivums and the less hardy agaves, echeverias and aeoniums scattered about in pots and on window sills. The kitchen garden and small orchard, which are across a meadow, nearer the cliffs, should on no account be missed. Those with no interest in vegetables will be recompensed by the spectacular view along the coast from Tintagel church to Lundy, and Port Isaac Bay and Pentire Point, even to Trevose headland.

open	Easter–end Oct, Wed pm, Sat am, pm; schools and groups by appointment
directions	SX43 58, Culver Road is near the town centre, and leads to the Town Quay
owner	Caradon District Council, leased to Tamar Protection Society
address	Mary Newman's Cottage, Culver Road, Saltash
enquiries	T: 01752 843388

EAST

SX43 58

size	0.2ha/0.5a
soil	Neutral
altitude	Near river level
aspect	In a SAGLV
rainfall	102–114cm/40–45in
temperature	Zone E

In 1568, when 17 years old, Mary Newman married Francis Drake at St Budeaux Church, Plymou where she lies buried. The tradition that she lived this house was already accepted by 1820, and th is no reason to believe otherwise. There had been dwellings here since the 12th century, although t present house appears to date from the 15th or 1 century, perhaps incorporating earlier material. T site has been described as originally a 'burgage ʀ – one on which vegetables might be grown and ɑ cow kept, customarily in size some 50 x 115ft (15 35m). The present garden is laid out in a typical ꞇ tage style of a much later date. It is divided into t sections – that nearest the house is a herb garden while the middle section is a lawn, with borders, an arbour from which there is a view of the river and its bridges. Indeed, it has been romantically suggested that from an upper window-seat in the cottage, Mary could have seen her husband's shiʀ rounding the headland into harbour. In the third tion, paths wind through beds of roses, herbaceoɵ and other plants, some, as the old-fashioned rose with appropriate names – 'Sir Walter Raleigh', an 'William Shakespeare', and a green santolina brought from Sudeley Castle, where it is said that Kathryn Parr had used the plant from her herb garden to ease Henry VIII's legs. The Cottage has been restored and is maintained by the Tamar Protection Society, and there are active plans to create an authentic Elizabethan merchant's garden here.

111 Mary Newman's Cottage

EAST

SX45 52

The commander of the Armada vowed he would over Mount Edgcumbe after victory and, by the century, it had become required viewing for pers of fashion, including Dr Johnson, Horace Walpo Samuel Pepys, and David Garrick. The Edgcumb while resident at **Cotehele** (102), first emparked here in 1515, only later moving residence, buildi a house unprotected and exposed to view, flaunt ing their high station. There is no illustration of t garden until that of Badeslade in 1737, which sh an elaborate and grand landscape. One part, laid as an amphitheatre of trees, was thought to have inspired Milton in describing the 'Walls of Paradi in his epic, so that a 'Temple of Milton' was built there. The 'Wilderness', near where the ferry now lands, was cut down in the 18th century, opening the way for the wife of the first Earl to lay out the English Garden, joined later by a French Garden, most elaborate of all, an Italian Garden with oran ery, fountain, and double steps with statues. Mor recently a geyser garden has been added to com

orate the family's
...ection with New
...and. All are open
...ew. Entrance to
...house is charged,
...s recommended
...e it includes the
...nstructed Earl's
...len. The Earl's
...leads to the
...ar Lawn with its
...lisite Shell Seat,
...usted with exotic
...ls believed to have
...n brought back
...aptain Cook, who
...n anchored in the
...below. Here too
...ne of the original
...trees planted in
...mid-16th century.

112 Mount Edgcumbe House & Country Park

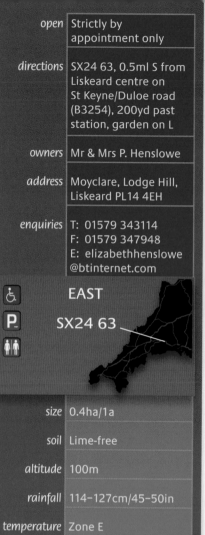

open	Strictly by appointment only
directions	SX24 63, 0.5ml S from Liskeard centre on St Keyne/Duloe road (B3254), 200yd past station, garden on L
owners	Mr & Mrs P. Henslowe
address	Moyclare, Lodge Hill, Liskeard PL14 4EH
enquiries	T: 01579 343114 F: 01579 347948 E: elizabethhenslowe@btinternet.com

EAST

SX24 63

size	0.4ha/1a
soil	Lime-free
altitude	100m
rainfall	114–127cm/45–50in
temperature	Zone E

Built in 1927 by Mrs Moira Reid and her husband, Moyclare takes its name from a combination of Moira and Co. Clare, where Mrs Reid was born. Although in a 'frost-pocket', by the 1970s the garden had reached its peak, becoming 'the most televised garden in Cornwall'. Mrs Reid was surprised and flattered to be asked to contribute to Alvilde Lees-Milne and Rosemary Verey's book *The Englishwoman's Garden*, although she had already written articles in the RHS *Journal*, and been visited by many celebrities, including Margery Fish, with whom she shared a love of variegated plants. A seed given her by J.C. Williams of **Caerhays** (71) became *Camellia williamsii* 'Moira Reid'; a *Eucalyptus gunnii* arrived as a gift from Beverley Nicholls, and John Betjeman was reprimanded for calling her Irish-woman's garden 'typically English'! In one article, 'Cramming them in', she wrote: 'I never want to see any bare earth at all'. This has created problems for Mrs Henslowe, who came to live here in 1997, after her aunt's death. Much was overgrown, and the more delicate plants were smothered. A rigorous programme of rehabilitation aims at retaining the spirit of the garden – its informality, with paths meandering through a succession of beds, making the garden appear larger than it is – but there are some new features. Two of these are a pergola covered with golden hop, and a rectangular pond bordered by astilbes. Louis Reid, Moira's husband, was a friend of the poet W.B. Yeats, and a line from his poem *He Wishes for the Cloths of Heaven*, peculiarly applicable to this garden, is inscribed on a memorial slate – 'Tread softly for you tread on my dreams'.

113 Moyclare

open	One Sun each, May, Jun, pm
directions	SX26 88, from Launceston St Stephen take road to Egloskerry. From centre of village entrance to Penheale is 0.5ml on R. Park in yard
owners	Mr & Mrs J. Colville
address	Penheale Manor, Launceston PL15 8RX
enquiries	T: 01566 785693 F: 01566 785762.
pronounced	penHEEL
EH	House: I; stables and gatehouse each I; dovecote II

EAST

SX26 88

EH	Walled garden with pavilions: II*, garden II
size	Medium size garden, in very large estate
soil	Lime-free
altitude	130–100m
aspect	E-sloping
rainfall	102–114cm/40–45in
temperature	Zone F
	Plant sales

The magnificent stables at Penheale were built by Sir John Specott in 1620, his son Paul completing the house on his marriage in 1636. The front court is entered through a remarkable gatehouse and loggia. Two similar courts above the house, enclosed by a wall, have pavilions at both ends and a raised walk. In 1867 a writer pronounced this to be 'one of the finest and best pre-served specimens of ancient manorial resi-dences in the county'. But by 1920, when it was acquired by Capt. Norman Colville, it was dilapidated. His admiration for Castle Drogo in Devon inspired him to engage Sir Edwin Lutyens to restore the house, and Lutyens also designed the parterre next to the house, when Gertrude Jekyll's advice was requested on the planting. The court-yard gardens were extended by the attach-ment of a square plat approximately four times their size. This similarly was quar-tered into four 'rooms' enclosed by high yew hedges, reminiscent of those at Castle Drogo. Along the house and extending to the full width of this plat, is a raised walk, lined both above and below by long her-baceous borders, designed by the late Mrs Colville and her gardener. At the end of a parallel grass path, midway between the four r_ of the parterre, steps lead down to a long lake _ canal, possibly created out of medieval stew p_ and ending in woodland planted with camellia_ rhododendrons. This insistent formality of squa_ and long axes is unique in Cornwall, and curio_ impressive, especially in conjunction with the c_ exceptional planting of the long herbaceous bo_ along the raised walk, the yew hedges by the h_ and at the far edge of the plat.

114 Penheale Manor Gardens

open	Groups by appointment
directions	SX21 62, from A38 at N end of Dobwalls follow the sign to Duloe, Herodsfoot and Looe for 1.5ml. Turn R at sign for Scawn; continue for 1ml down to the river
owners	Mrs A. Ball & Dr Julian Ball
address	Scawn Mill, nr Liskeard PL14 4GS
enquiries	T: 01579 320497

P

☕

EAST

SX21 62

size	Medium
soil	Lime-free
altitude	65m
aspect	In a SAGLV
rainfall	114–127cm/45–50in
temperature	Zone E
	Plant sales

The Corn Mill around which the present garden has been created dates back 300 years. Water was taken from the West Looe river to be fed into two mill-pools to drive the wheel. The mill was rebuilt at least twice in its lifetime, but fell into disuse and disrepair after the 1920s, until the more recent partial restoration of the building. Over the years two new woodlands have been planted – the more distant Larch Wood replaced that of scrub oak in 1964; the Penpoly Wood leading from the house was planted in 1992, from a mixture of 7,000 beech and Scotch pine seeds. Around the house are various areas of planting, begun in 1977 – a tennis court below the house, and a Japanese garden leading into the wood. On the other side of the road are a croquet lawn and a fish pond, leading on through woodland underplanted with candelabra primulas to the lake by the larch wood. This was dug down to rock level and waterproofed. A path runs around the lake, which has been planted with Japanese flowering cherrie azaleas and rhododendrons, bamboos and pines, each making their contribution throughout the sea sons to the picturesque reflections in the still wate of the lake.

115 Scawn Mill

open	One Sun each Mar, May and Aug, am, pm for NGS, and by appointment
directions	SX20 99, 5ml S of Bude off A39 at Bangors Cross Roads (chapel on corner). Turn into Vicarage Lane, signed to Poundstock church, *c.*200yd on L
owners	Mr P.R. & Mrs J.A. Marfleet
address	Southfield, Vicarage Lane, Poundstock EX23 0AU
enquiries	T: 01288 361233

EAST

SX20 99

size	1.25ha/3a
soil	Lime-free
altitude	100m
aspect	S-sloping, in an AONB
rainfall	102–114cm/40–45in
temperature	Zone E
	Plant sales

In an earlier guise, Southfield featured a collection of some 40 minority breed of fowl, with pigs and goats, which eventually attracted 10,000 visitors a year. This was brought to a sudden halt by the notorious salmonella and listeria scare of 1994, even though there were no cases in Cornwall. Mr and Mrs Marfleet, forced to retrench, began to recreate their land into a garden. The bungalow faces south over a sloping lawn with a terrace, pond and small bed in front, from which there is a fine view of the surrounding countryside. A large herbaceous border down the left side of the garden divides off the kitchen garden, which runs the whole length of the lawn. This is

matched on the other side of the lawn by an orch of fruit trees, among which is the old-fashioned medlar. At the bottom left-hand corner of the law an arch covered with golden hop leads out into a plantation stretching the whole width of the uppe garden, in which there is a wide variety of native trees – several forms of oak, beech, rowan, and spindle among others. Beyond this the plantation grades down into natural woodland above a strea Where the path winds around the tree collection, is bordered by an underplanting of rhododendroi and other shrubs. In particular, distributed along sides are 22 distinct varieties of hydrangeas, whi make a colourful spectacle, especially where the turns into a small glade. Alongside the varied inte in this garden is the added attraction of home-ma produce on sale, and, when open all day, the opp tunity for a light lunch.

116 Southfield

open	One Sun each in May, Jun, Sep, but strictly not open to the public at any other time
directions	SX26 77, near junction of B3254 and B3257
owners	The Latham family
address	Trebartha, North Hill, near Launceston PL15 7PD
pronounced	treBARTHa
EH	Barton: II*

EAST

SX26 77 _____

size	Very large estate
soil	Lime-free
altitude	250–130m
aspect	E-sloping, in an AONB
rainfall	127–152cm/50–60in
temperature	Zone F

A sketch of about 1690 shows Trebartha with an elaborate garden full of statues in an Italianate st This was swept away in the 18th century by Col. Rodd, who erected on its site what Gilbert con- sidered 'a large tasteless building', although with 'good gardens ... surrounded by extensive planta tions' through which a torrent roared down from moors above. Trebartha found a place in Loudon gazetteer of 1822, and 50 years later was describ as 'the best and most stately seat in the county'. I was these plantations, probably planted by Franc Hearle Rodd in the early 19th century, which led Latham family in 1941 – a time of import shortag – to take advantage of the timber, by purchasing property. The 'American Gardens' and Upper Terr were probably mid-19th-century, when many new varieties were becoming available from plant coll tors. The Swan Pool, whose boathouse has recen been restored, is landscaped with other interestin specimens, and dates from the beginning of the

117 Trebartha

century. A mound of earth over a
by grotto-like cave serves as a Mount
iewing the lake. The house, maligned by Gilbert,
me delapidated during occupation in the Second
d War, and was demolished in 1948. A well in the
parkland has been surrounded by a collection
ncient crosses and mile-stones. In 2001, a millen-
n plantation was created with a range of interesting
ng broadleaf trees and conifers. There has been ex-
ive clearing and replanting of trees and shrubs on
Victorian terraces, opening up a number of scenic
vs across the surrounding area. The word 'magical'
become a cliché when applied to Cornish gardens,
the stillness of the Swan Pool, broken only by the
ant roar of the torrent and the sighing of the great
s that tower up the slopes above, induces an atmos-
re to which this over-used word is not inapplicable.
bartha is a private estate, open only on charity days,
in which there are no rights of way.

open	Mid-May–end Jun groups of 10+ by appointment, pm or evening
directions	SX33 84, follow signs for Leisure Centre along Dunheved Rd. At College end of road take sharp L bend; immediately after, take another L turn into Windmill Hill. Trenance is c.200yd on L. Park in road
owners	Mr & Mrs John Dingle
address	Trenance, Windmill Hill, Launceston PL15 9AG
enquiries	T: 01566 772067
pronounced	treNANCE

EAST

SX33 84

size	0.5ha/1.75a
soil	Lime-free
altitude	180m
rainfall	102–114cm/40–45in
temperature	Zone G
	Plant sales

The two acres (0.8ha) at Trenance form an unusu ally large garden for a town house, although in a road where there are other large gardens. Windm Hill, as its name implies, is high above the town, and the entrance to the house, lined with mature rhododendrons and camellias, opens up a vista to the countryside beyond. The sloping site has been terraced and planted to provide interest througho the year. Above the house is a lawned area with a long herbaceous border, a small 'cottage garden', and a collection of hollies. Opposite the house is a formal courtyard garden. Below are a series of gardens surrounding a lawn tennis court, includi herbaceous beds and borders, an enclosed slated garden of colourful perennials, an area of heathe and conifers, and a 'winter border'. Ballard *Helleb* are a speciality of Trenance, as are hardy geraniu of which there are over 100 varieties distributed throughout the garden.

118 Trenance

open	Two Suns for NGS, pm
directions	SX38 58, from Saltash take A38. Turn L towards Trematon. Through village, take R fork. Take 2nd lane on R. After 0.25ml take entrance on R
owners	Gloria and John Lankshear
address	Trevollard Farm, nr Trematon, Saltash PL12 4 RX
enquiries	T: 01752 842347 E: glankshear@ plym.ac.uk
pronounced	treVOLLard

EAST

SX38 58

size	1.62ha/4a
soil	Mixed and neutral
altitude	85m
aspect	Many dimensional, in an AONB
rainfall	89 –103cm/35–40in
temperature	Zone D
	Plant sales

Trevollard Farm is situated in the countryside above the Lynher Valley. When John and Gloria Lankshear finished farming, they converted one of their barns into a house and retained some of the fields to create a garden. The land is divided into a number of areas with very different characteristics. One is now a thriving and densely planted arboretum, which still allows glimpses down to the river. Another has a long herbaceous border stocked with a wide variety of plants, many of them donated by friends, and others grown in the greenhouses in abundant quantities by Gloria's father. The rose Rambling Rector scrambles over a nearby pergola at the centre of the gooseberries, raspberries, blackcurrants and loganberries in the fruit garden. In the shelter of mature trees are two circular garden rooms, one dominated by a large circular flowerbed, regularly filled with pansies and sweet-williams. In the second 'room', a mysterious atmosphere is created by a number of granite sto upended to form a circle.

Beside the house is a sheltered sitting space – a pebbled courtyard, the back wall covered with creeper and a passionflower, heavily laden with blooms and fruits in season. A loggia supports a v that bears numerous bunches of grapes. Steps lea up to another spacious lawn overlooking a sweep of open countryside. A living sculpture of willows being grown at one end. The layered willow hedg kept low to preserve the view, and a summerhous strategically sited higher up to take advantage of sunsets.

open	One weekend in Jul for NGS, pm
directions	SX09 90, from Camelford take B3266 N. On outskirts of Boscastle park as directed and proceed on foot
owners	Alex and Ian Stewart
address	Wildwood, Doctor's Hill, Boscastle PL35 0BA
enquiries	T: 01840 250316

EAST

SX09 90

size	0.4ha/1a
soil	Acid
altitude	100m
aspect	S, in an AONB
rainfall	102–114cm/40–45in
temperature	Zone E

Wildwood, on the steep hillside overlooking Boscastle, was one of the areas that suffered in the dramatic flooding of 2004. The water coursed through the higher garden, flattening plants and sweeping away structures before pouring into the house. By the following summer, however, a huge amount of hard work had brought about a substantial restoration. The south-facing terrace is again a peaceful area, where a vivid red campsis rambles across the wall and reaches on to the roof. Neat lawns in the formal garden are once more surrounded by colourful shrubberies, and a dovecote stands over a secluded corner. When the Stewarts moved into the brand new house in 1991, they found the immediate surroundings without topsoil, so much heavy work was required to create beds and build steps to the upper levels. Stones were crowbarred out of the ground and used for walling, and Alex grew on seedlings and cuttings for much of the planting. Young specimen trees have been sited in the upper lawns. Higher up, the woodland area contains mature trees that provide shelter from all but the north winds, and give welcome shade in summer. The varied underplanting includes numerous tree ferns, phoenix and dracaena palms, and bamboos. A paulownia grown from se stands near a banana plant, and a striking impres sion is made by *Phytolacca americana* – the Amer. pokeweed. The shady pond is now filled by rainw ter, as the original feed from the nearby river was disrupted by the floodwater.

120 Wildwood

This book is a guide to gardens that are reliably open to the public. However, there are a substantial number of fine gardens in Cornwall that open occasionally, but not on a regular basis. Among these are more than half the gardens listed by English Heritage as of national significance, and all but two of the gardens for which Humphry Repton produced Red Books between 1792 and 1810. They are therefore mentioned below, out of general interest, and in order to complete the gazetteer. However, the question arises, 'How can I know when they will be open?' There is no simple answer. Typically, these gardens open for chari-

and to listen to local radio programme. The diocesan monthly *The Coracle*; the monthly magazine *Inside Cornwall*, and the two free papers *The Cornish Countr* *Gardener* and *The Cornish Gardener*, wh can be found in nurseries, all contain u to-date information.

For the purposes of cross-reference, these gardens are numbered in sequer with those in the main gazetteer.

121 Carclew
SW78 38 Perranarworthal

Carclew (above) originally belonged to the Daunger family. In 1749 it was sold to William Lemon, and Thomas Edwar of Greenwich designed 'one of the most ... elegant buildings [in] the county'. Lemon' grandson, Sir William Lemon was principally responsible for laying out the garden and grounds, followed by his son Sir Charle whose gardener William Beattie Booth was a notable horticulturist. Sir Charles was a keen plant collector, encouraging the Packet commanders to introduce

6 Historic Gardens Open Occasionally

ties, parish festivals or other occasions, which are generally advertised only locally, and perhaps not long in advance. Those wishing to visit such gardens are advised to keep a watch on local papers,

plants; sponsoring Joseph Hooker's
alayan expedition, and engaging as
ekeeper the father of William and
mas Lobb, the great Cornish plant
ters. Lemon's brother-in-law, John
rle Tremayne of the Heligan family,
tinued the gardening tradition.
arclew was among the ten gardens in
don's gazetteer of 1822, and featured
9th-century horticultural journals.
 main gardens are arranged around
'Higher Pond' above the 'Wheel
d', where many fine rhododendrons,
h as *falconeri*, and the original Luco-
e oaks are to be found. The present
se, built in 1963, replaced a magnifi-
t dwelling burnt down in 1934.
he estate is now divided among
aller residences and farms, but the
ater part of the historic garden
vives intact. The garden is EH-listed
de II, and has opened until recently.

2 Catchfrench Manor
0 59 St Germans

chfrench probably derived its name
m the Norman French *chasse franche* –
e warren' – in the 13th century, when
 Cornish purchased from the king the
ht to hunt. Repton was introduced to
ncis Glanville, an MP of William Pitt's
ty, by Richard Pole Carew of **Antony**
). He recommended plantations to give
vacy to the house, and the opening
 of a prospect by the removal of earth.
e garden is EH-listed Grade II, and
s been open until a recent change of
nership.

3 Chyverton
79 51 Zelah

yverton was listed EH II after it was
ognized as a classic 18th-century
dscape – unusual in Cornwall – with a
dge over a serpentine lake, and a Folly

as an eye-catcher, originally 'Hunter's
Lodge', but later separated as a residence
then known as 'Tinker's Castle'. In recent
years, since it was purchased in 1924 by
Treve Holman, it has become renowned
for its trees and shrubs, many collected
and introduced by his son Nigel. It is
particularly well known for its magnolias. Open 1 March to 30 May to groups,
strictly by appointment.
(T: 01872 540324.)

124 The Downes
SW55 36 Trelissick Road, Hayle
The Downes was designed by Edmund
Sedding, and the garden by his brother
John Dando Sedding, author of *Garden
Craft Old and New* (1891), a book that
influenced both Thomas Mawson and
Edwin Lutyens. It is EH-listed Grade II,
as the only surviving work of this high
Victorian designer's style. The Downes
has been the convent of a nursing order
in association with St Michael's Hospital,
but has recently been sold.

125 Lamellen
SX05 77 St Tudy
The house at Lamellen, a Domesday
manor, was built in 1849 by John Pen-

267

berthy Magor, but it was his son, E.J.P. Magor, who in 1901 seriously applied himself to gardening there, obtaining seed from E.H. Wilson's expeditions and himself joining Reginald Farrer collecting Alpines in Switzerland. He was celebrated for his many rhododendron hybrids, especially between Himalayan species – 'Damaris' and 'Lamellen' probably being the best. His son, Maj. Walter Magor, followed his lead, becoming editor of the *Rhododendron Yearbook*, and chairman of the RHS Rhododendron and Camellia Group, receiving the Veitch Memorial Medal in 1987. Lamellen (above) is EH-listed Grade II, and is still well maintained by the family.

126 Menabilly
SX10 51   near Fowey

Menabilly is the principal seat of the Rashleigh family of Fowey, and in 1822 the garden was described in the gazetteer in Loudon's *Encyclopoedia* as a 'showplace'. It was the model for 'Manderley' in Daphne du Maurier's novel *Rebecca*, and for a time she resided here. It was once celebrated for its collection of bamboos – 'probably as comprehensive as any in

the country'; its rare conifers, some from Kew, in 'Hooker Grove'; and a grotto garnished with specimens of Cornish minerals. Menabilly is EH-listed Grade I and long-term regeneration plans are in hand.

127 Pentillie Castle
SX40 64   Pillaton

Pentillie – a castellated house, never a castle – overlooks the River Tamar. Repton, who visited here on the recommendation of Pole Carew of **Antony** (99), admitted in his Red Book of 1810 that he was unfamiliar with this type of terrain. The major outcome from his visit was the remodelling of the house by his associate, William Wilkins, in an 'ecclesiastically Gothic style', possibly with assistance from his son. These additions were demolished in 1968. Loudon included Pentillie in his *Encyclopoedia* gazetteer of 1822. It is EH-listed Grade II, and has been opened, but not recently.

128 Port Eliot
SX35 57   St Germans

Port Eliot was the first estate in Cornwall to be visited by Humphry Repton in

)2, by reason of Eliot's relationship
marriage to William Pitt the younger,
o had consulted him in 1791. Repton
gested in his Red Book that the house
ght be joined to the Abbey; this and
ny other of his recommendations were
taken up, but reappeared in some
he proposals of Sir John Soane for
house. There are also sketches for
erations to the garden thought to be
W.S. Gilpin, but never followed. Port
t appears in the gazetteer of Loudon's
yclopoedia as a 'show-place', and is
-listed Grade I. This garden is open by
itation only.

) Trehane
86 48 Probus

e Trehane family, already considered
cient' in 1288, remained in possession
he barton until the mid-17th century.
he 19th century, the estate came into
possession of Captain William Stack-
se Church Pinwill, a notable horticul-
st who was awarded the RHS Victoria
dal. From 1888 to 1900 there were
ught to be 4,500 species growing in
garden, the majority of them herba-
us. The mansion was regarded as one
he most beautiful in Cornwall until it
s gutted by fire in 1943. In 1963 the
ate came into the ownership of David
hane, a descendant of a branch of the
ginal family. He was a leading author-
in the country on camellias. The cur-
t owner hopes to restore the mansion
subsequently make arrangements for
pening the garden.

) Trewarthenick
90 44 Tregony

warthenick was visited by Humphry
ton during his excursion in 1792,
which he produced his Red Book in
3. His recommendations for separat-

ing the farm from the house approach;
for hiding the service buildings, and
breaking up the central avenue have
generally been followed. Nevertheless, Trewarthenick remains a forgotten
garden, even though it is EH-listed Grade
II. It has since developed and is being
maintained, and has been opened, but
not recently.

131 Werrington Park
SX33 87 near Launceston

Werrington (below) is important first because there is circumstantial evidence for
the influence of William Kent by way of
Nicholas Morice's marriage to Catherine,
daughter of the Earl of Pembroke, who
was active in the Palladian circle. There
was a Palladian-style bridge; a ruined

castle; a temple of the sun; a triumphal
arch 'on the model of that on Sidon Hill
at Highclere'; a hermitage 'like that at
Richmond', and a reproduction of the
Tomb of the Horatii at Albano. Most of
these have gone or are ruinous. Later, after its purchase by J.C. Williams of **Caerhays** (71) in 1882, Werrington became
a repository for the overflow especially
of rhododendrons received from expeditions supported by the family, particularly
those of Forrest. The garden is EH-listed
Grade II, and opens occasionally.

Cornwall is well supplied with nurseries, several of which specialize in varieties of plants that may be difficult to find elsewhere. However, this list provides as wide a conspectus as possible of what is available from one end of the county to the other. It is divided into three sections:

1 *Garden centres*, which supply a variety of gardening and leisure items, as well as plants.

2 *Nurseries associated with the gardens in the Guide*, where further information will be found. Most gardens sell plants when they are open, but those listed are permanent nurseries, open to the public even when not visiting the garden. Among them, 'plant centres' are smaller than 'nurseries', which in some cases are substantial.

3 *Plant nurseries*, whose focus is upon plants rather than horticultural necessities.

Nurseries & Garden Centres

The garden centres and nurseries that are asterisked are those which contribute to the *RHS Plant Finder*. Note that the garden nurseries feature strongly in this context. It is not possible here to include descriptions of all the nurseries, but where notes are added it is in order to identify those that specialize.

1 Garden centres

Brooks Garden Centre, Stratton, Bude EX23 9NR. T: 01288 352897. F: 01288 356159. E: brooks.gardencentre@virgin.net W: www.brooksgardencentre.co.uk

Camborne Garden Centre, North Roske Terrace, Camborne TR14 8PR. T/F: 01209 613819.

Carnon Downs Garden Centre, Quenchwell Road, Carnon Downs, Truro TR3 6LN. T: 01872 863058. F: 01872 862162.

Chacewater Garden Centre, Three Milestone Road, Chacewater, Truro TR4 8QG. T/F: 01872 560533.

Falmouth Garden Centre, Swanpool Road, Goldenbank, Falmouth TR11 5BH. T/F: 01326 315404. E: falgc@freeserve.co.uk

Goldenbank Nursery & Garden Centre, Plymouth Road, Liskeard PL14 3PB. T/F: 01579 348622.

Goonhavern Garden Centre, Newquay Road, Goonhavern, Truro TR4 9QQ. T: 01872 575088. F: 01872 575097.

Homeleigh Garden Centre, Dutson, Launceston PL15 9SP. T: 01566 773147. F: 01566 773547. E: sales@homeleighgardencentre.co.u W: www.homeleighgardencentre.co.u

Looe Garden Centre, St Martin Looe PL13 1HX. T: 01503 263866

Newquay Garden Centre, Quintrell Downs, Newquay TF 4LG. T/F: 01637 872199.

Pengelly Plant Centre, Hewas Water, St Austell PL26 7JG. T: 01726 883757 F: 01726 882428.

Rising Sun Nurseries Plant & Garden Centre, Harrowbarrow, Callington PL 8JD. T/F: 01579 351231. W: www.risingsunnurseries.co.uk

St Austell Garden Centre, Boscundle, St Austell PL25 3RJ. T: 01726 812197 F: 01726 812282. E: garden@wtltd.co.uk

Tamar View Nurseries & Garden Centre Ltd., Callington Road, Carkeel

ltash PL12 6PH. T: 01752 847366.
01752 840992.
awney Garden Leisure, Sladesbridge,
adebridge PL27 6JA.
01208 893030. F: 01208 814798.
enquiries@trelawney.co.uk
: www.trelawney.co.uk
sillian Garden Centre, Tresillian, Truro
R2 4BA. T/F: 01872 520544.
evena Cross Nurseries & Garden
entre, Breage, Helston TR13 9PS.
01736 763880. F: 01736 762828.
sales@trevenacross.co.uk
: www.trevenacross.co.uk *Speciality:*
outh African and Australasian plants
aloes, proteas (largest grower in the
K), tree ferns, palms, restios – wide
nge of other plants and hardy exotics
vassack Nurseries Garden Centre,
igh Lanes, Hayle. T/F: 01736 752119.
venson Moor Garden Centre, Cross
oads, Tehidy, Camborne TR14 0EP.
/F: 01209 610909.
evale Garden Centres plc: Lelant,
ut Lane, Hayle TR27 6LG. T: 01736
53731. W: www.wyevale.co.uk
evale Garden Centres plc: St Austell,
ar Moor Road, St Austell PL24 2SQ.
: 01726 814854. F: 01726 814253.
': www.wyevale.co.uk

Nurseries associated with gardens

osvigo (39), Bosvigo Lane, Truro,
R1 3NH. T: 01872 275774. F: 01872
75774. E: bosvigo.plants@virgin.net
/: www.bosvigo.com
urncoose Nurseries (7), Gwennap,
edruth TR16 6BJ. T: 01209 860316.
: 01209 860011.
: info@burncoose.co.uk
/: www.burncoose.co.uk
xtensive range of over 3,000 ornamen-
al trees and shrubs. Rare and unusual
agnolias and rhododendrons
winion Bamboo Garden (40), Mawnan

Smith, Falmouth TR11 5JA. T: 01326
250258. F: 01326 250903.
Speciality: bamboos
Cotehele Plant Centre (102), nr Saltash.
Glendurgan Plant Centre (43), Mawnan
Smith.
Heligan Gardens Ltd. (81), The Lost
Gardens of Heligan, nr St Austell.
Hidden Valley Gardens & Nurseries (76),
Treesmill, Par PL24 2TU. T: 01208
873225.
E: hiddenvalleygardens@yahoo.co.uk
W: www.hiddenvalleygardens.co.uk
Speciality: Siberian iris, crocosmias, hardy
geraniums, and soft fruit
Japanese Garden & Bonsai Nursery (77),
St Mawgan, Newquay TR8 4ET.
T: 01637 860116. F: 01637 860887.
E: rob@thebonsainursery.com
W: www.thebonsainursery.com
*Lanhydrock Plant Nursery (79), Bodmin
PL30 5AD. T: 01208 265950. F: 01208
265959. E: lanhydrock@nationaltrust.
org.uk. W: www.nationaltrust.org.uk
*Pine Lodge Nursery (87), Holmbush,
St Austell PL25 3RQ. T: 01726 73500.
F: 01726 77370.
E: garden@pine-lodge.com
W: www.pine-lodge.co.uk
Pinsla Garden & Nursery (88), Cardin-
ham, Bodmin PL30 4AY. T/F: 01208
821339. E: info@pinslagarden.co.uk
W: www.pinslagarden.co.uk
*Roseland House Nursery (21),
Chacewater, Truro TR4 8QB.
T: 01872 560451.
E: clematis@roselandhouse.co.uk
Speciality: climbing plants
*Trebah Enterprises Ltd. (58), Mawnan
Smith, Falmouth TR11 5JZ.
T: 01326 250448. F: 01326 250781.
E: mail@trebah-garden.co.uk
W: www.trebah-garden.co.uk
*Tregothnan Nursery (60), Estate
Office, Tregothnan, Truro TR2 4AN.

T: 01872 520325. F: 01872 520291.
E: bigplants@tregothnan.com
W: www.tregothnan.com
Speciality: rare and unusual plants from own stock, with known-provenance, large specimens
Tregrehan (95), Par. T: 01726 814389.
Speciality: wild source material and camellias
Trelissick Plant Centre (61), Feock
Trelowarren Plant Centre (29), Mawgan
Trengwainton Plant Centre (30), Penzance
*****Trewithen Nurseries** (65), Grampound Road, Truro TR2 4DD. T: 01726 882764. F: 01726 882301. E: gardens@trewithen-estate.demon.co.uk W: www.trewithengardens.co.uk

3   Plant nurseries

Note: Nurseries listed without postcodes do not usually trade by mail order.
Badgers Holt Nursery, Mount Whistle, Ashton, Helston.
*****Barracott Plants**, Old Orchard, Calstock Road, Gunnislake PL18 9AA. T/F: 01822 832234.
E: geoff@geoff63.freeserve.co.uk
W: www.barracottplants.co.uk
Herbaceous perennials, especially shade-loving plants
Blackacre Nurseries, Blackacre, nr Indian Queens. T/F: 01637 881300.
*****Bodmin Plant & Herb Nursery**, Laveddon Mill, Bodmin. T: 01208 72837. F: 01208 76491.
E: bodminnursery@aol.com
*****Bregover Plants**, Hillbrooke, Middlewood, North Hill, nr Launceston PL15 7NN. T: 01566 782661. *Unusual hardy herbaceous perennials*
Brighton Cross Plant Centre, Grampound Road, Truro. T: 01726 882807
Brown's Nurseries, Trewidland, Liskeard. T: 01503 240373. F: 01503 240670.

Calamazag Nursery, East Taphouse, Liskeard. T/F: 01579 321799
Cedar Croft Nurseries, Hengar Lane, St Tudy, Bodmin. T: 01208 851072. F: 01208 851552.
*****Churchtown Nurseries**, Gulval, Penzance. T/F: 01736 362626. *Speciality perennials, grasses and restios*
Churchtown Nursery, Perranarwortha nr Truro. T: 01872 863033. *Speciality snowdrops (over 100 varieties), outdoor hardy plants and fruit trees*
Cornish Garden Nurseries, Perranarworthal, nr Truro. T: 01872 864380.
Cross Common Nursery, The Lizard, Helston TR12 7PD. T/F: 01326 2907
E: info@crosscommonnursery.co.uk
W: www.crosscommonnursery.co.uk
Half-hardy, exotic and conservatory plants; plants for coastal gardens, citr olives and grapes
*****The Duchy of Cornwall Nursery**, Cot Road, Lostwithiel PL22 0HW. T: 0120 872668. F: 01208 872835.
E: sales@duchynursery.co.uk
W: www.duchyofcornwallnursery.co.
Very wide range of all garden plants, including trees, shrubs, conifers, roses, perennials, fruit, and half-hardy exotic
Fentongollen Bulb Farm, Merther Lan Tresillian, Truro TR2 4AQ.
T: 01872 520209. F: 01872 520606.
E: bulbs@flowerfarm.co.uk
W: www.flowerfarm.co.uk. *Bulb sales Aug–Dec*
*****Fir Tree Farm Nursery**, Tresahor, Constantine, Falmouth TR11 5PL.
T: 01326 340593.
E: plants@cornwallgardens.com
W: www.cornwallgardens.com
4,200 different perennials, and 80 clematis
Fiveways Nursery, Pelean Cross, Ponsanooth, Truro. T/F: 01872 8651
Glen Carne Nursery, Glen Carne, Barkl

op, St Agnes. T/F: 01872 552446.
eciality: hanging baskets and tubs
olphin Hill Nursery, Godolphin,
elston TR13 9TQ. T/F: 01736 762124.
vicki@godolphinhill.com
': www.godolphinhill.com
eciality: old-fashioned and species
ses, and herbs
en Lane Nursery, Green Lane,
edruth. T/F: 01209 313245.
newseason@lineone.net
': www.newseasonltd.com
ring bedding, shrubs, cottage garden
ants, organically grown
eek Nurseries, Parc Bottom, Gweek,
elston. T: 01326 221311.
rdy Exotics Nursery, Gilly Lane,
hitecross, Penzance TR20 8BZ.
01736 740660. F: 01736 741101.
contact@hardyexotics.co.uk
': www.hardyexotics.co.uk. Largest UK
llection of trees, shrubs and herbaceous
ants for tropical and desert effects
ather Lane Nursery, Back Lane,
anonstown, Penzance. T/F: 01736
40198.
nd Nurseries, Illand, Coads Green,
aunceston. T: 01566 782521.
Carniverous Plants, 27 St Michael's
oad, Ponsanooth, Truro TR3 7ED.
: 01872 863391. Carniverous plants
nly
. Nursery, Rosenannon, St Wenn,
r Bodmin. T: 01637 880108.
helland Horticultural Centre Ltd.,
elhelland, Camborne. T: 01209
12445. F: 01209 718975.
: enquiries@kelhellandhort.co.uk
': www.kelhellandhort.co.uk
jeth Nurseries, Coombe Rd, Lanjeth,
t Austell PL26 7TL. T/F: 01726 77973.
re Nursery, Ruan High Lanes,
r Truro. T/F: 01872 501502.
wer Kenneggy Nurseries, Rosudgeon,
enzance. T: 01736 762959. Speciality:

plants for coastal gardens, Australasian
and South African plants, especially
agapanthus, kniphofia, agaves and other
succulents
Medrow Nursery, Polyphant, Launceston.
T: 01566 86322. Speciality: fruit and
vegetables, bedding plants, and trees
Michaelstow Nurseries, St Tudy, Bodmin.
T: 01208 851262.
Myrtle Nursery, High Lane, Manaccan.
T: 01326 231604.
*The Old Withy Garden Nursery,
The Grange Fruit Farm, Gweek, Helston
TR12 6BE. T: 01326 221171.
E: WithyNursery@fsbdial.co.uk
Pentewan Valley Nurseries, Pentewan
Road, St Austell. T/F: 01726 842360.
Penventon Nursery, Cumford, Lanner,
Redruth. T/F: 01209 820049.
E: info@penventonnursery.co.uk
Plantation Nursery, Botetoe Road, Barip-
per, nr Camborne. T/F: 01209 714522.
ProperPlants.com, Penknight, Lostwithiel
PL22 0JD. T/F: 01208 872291. Ring for
opening times.
E: info@ProperPlants.com
W: www.ProperPlants.com
Speciality: Herbaceous perennials, and
unusual herbs, grasses and ferns
*Quality Daffodils, 14 Roscarrack Close,
Falmouth TR11 4PJ. T/F: 01326
317959. E: rascamp@daffodils.uk.com
W: www.qualitydaffodils.co.uk
Speciality: narcissus hybrids and species.
Mail order only
Rainbow's End Nuseries, Rocky Lane,
Trescowe Common, nr Penzance.
T/F: 01736 850322.
*Rezare Nurseries, Rezare, nr Trebur-
ley, Launceston PL15 9NX. T: 01579
370969. E: rezarenurseries@aol.com
*Rosewarne Collections, Duchy College,
Rosewarne, Camborne.
T: 01209 722161. F: 01209 722159.
E: marshall.hutchens@duchy.ac.uk.

W: www.cornwall.ac.uk/duchy
Speciality: National Collection of escallonia hybrids and species
St Kitts Herbery, Starrapark, Camelford PL32 9XH. T: 01840 213442.
E: enquiries@stkittsherbery.co.uk.
Speciality: herbs
Sunny Corner Nurseries, Old Market Garden Centre, Chacewater, Truro. T/F: 01872 560084.
E: helen@sunny-corner.co.uk
W: www.sunny-corner.co.uk
Tarten Down Nurseries, Landrake, Saltash. T: 01752 851431.
Top Orchard Nurseries, Top Orchard Barn, Gulval, Penzance TR18 3BG. T: 01736 332430. F: 01736 331016.
Speciality: lilies. Mail order only
Towan Camellias, Carwinion Garden, Mawnan Smith, Falmouth. T/F: 01326 251115.
E: johnp@towancamellias.go-plus.net
*****Trecanna Nursery**, Latchley, nr Gunnislake PL18 9AX. T: 01822 834680.
E: mark@trecanna.com
W: www.trecanna.com
Speciality: unusual bulbs, perennials and South African plants, especially crocosmias and eucomis
*****Tregothnan Nursery**, see above under *Nurseries associated with gardens.*
Trenowth Nurseries, Lower Trenowth Bungalow, St Columb. T: 01637 881473.
Speciality: bedding plants, hanging baskets, and tubs. Open Apr-Jun
Treseders, Wallcottage Nurseries, Lockengate, St Austell. T: 01208 832234. E: Treseders@btconnect.com
*****Tresidder Farm Plants**, St Buryan, Penzance TR19 6EZ. T: 01736 810656.
E: niallmilligan@gmail.com
Speciality: Proteaceae, Aloeacae – large aloe collection, unusual succulents. Mail order only
*****Trevena Cross Nurseries**, Breage, nr

Helston, *see above under Garden centr*
West Coast Gardens, Dorminack, St Buryan, Penzance TR19 6BH.
T/F: 01736 810087. *Plants of Cornish origin; coastal garden plants, ferns and historic daffodils. Mail order only*
*****Winchester Growers Ltd.**, Varfell Farm Long Rock, Penzance TR20 8AQ.
T: 01736 851033.
E: dahlias@wgltd.co.uk
W: www.wgltd.co.uk
Speciality: dahlias as rooted cuttings

Gardens open all year

ey Gardens (1), Tresco, Isles of Scilly
a House (101), Poundstock, *most Sats
d Suns*
bara Hepworth Museum & Sculpture
rden (4), St Ives
awen Park (38), Truro
ncoose (7), nr Redruth, *excluding
ristmas*
eg Dhu (2), St Mary's, Isles of Scilly
vinion (40), Mawnan Smith
hele (102), St Dominick, Saltash
n Project (73), nr St Austell, *excluding
, 25 Dec*
Rosehill (42), Falmouth
olphin Estate (12), nr Helston, *for
lks*
yngdune (45), Falmouth
d Gardens (3), Tresco
nese Garden (77), St Mawgan,
luding 25 Dec–1 Jan*
berley Park (47), Falmouth
hydrock (79), nr Bodmin
terns (50), Mylor
g Cross (80), nr Port Isaac
Gardens
Heligan
), nr
Austell,
luding*
, 25 Dec*
acuddle (84), St Austell
rab Gardens (14), Penzance
nt Edgcumbe (112), Maker, *park
clare (113), Liskeard, *strictly by
pointment only*
adise Park (15), Hayle
gersick Castle (16), Praa Sands, *by
pointment*
lee Memorial Gardens (17), Penzance
rose (18), Hayle, *for walks*
e Lodge (87), nr St Austell, *daily,
luding 24–26 Dec*
gwynne (53), Feock, *by appointment
ly*

Queen Mary Gardens (54), Falmouth
Roskillys (22), St Keverne
St Just-in-Roseland Churchyard (55),
    St Just-in-Roseland
Scawn Mill (115), Liskeard, *by appointment*
Scorrier House (25), Scorrier, *strictly by
    appointment only*
Tehidy (26), Portreath, nr Redruth
Trebah (58), Mawnan Smith
Tregenna Castle (27), St Ives
Tregothnan (60), nr Truro, *strictly by
    appointment only*
Tregullow (28), Redruth, *by appointment*
Trelissick (61), Feock, *excluding 23–27
    Dec*
Tremough (62), Penryn, *by appointment*
Trenance Gardens (96), Newquay
Tresco Abbey Gardens (1), Isles of Scilly
Tresillian House (98), nr Newquay, *groups
    by appointment only*
Trevarno (32), nr Helston, *excluding 25,
    26 Dec*
Trewoofe Orchard (35), Lamorna, *by
    appointment*
Victoria Park (67), Truro

Calendar of Garden Openings

2 Gardens open in spring and summer

Antony House (99), Torpoint, *Apr–
    Oct, Tue–Thu; also bank holiday Mons
    and Suns Jun–Aug*
Antony Woodland (100), Torpoint,
    *Mar–Oct, excluding Mons and Fris except
    bank holidays*
Bonython (5), nr Helston, *mid-Apr–mid-
    Sep, Tue–Fri*
Bosahan (6), Manaccan, *Mar–Sep, by
    appointment only*
Bosvigo (39), Truro, *Mar–Sep, Thur–Fri*
Caerhays Castle (71), Gorran, *mid-Feb–
    end summer*

275

Chygurno (9), Lamorna, *Apr–May, Wed; Jul–Aug, Wed, Sun, and by appointment*
Chyverton (123), Zelah, *Mar–May, groups strictly by appointment only*
Creed House (72), Grampound, *Feb–Oct*
Enys (41), Mylor, *Mar–Oct, 1st Sun in month, Tue, Thu*
Flambards (11), Helston, *Easter–Oct, see note for exceptions in low season*
Gillhouse (104), nr St Neot, *Apr–Jul, by appointment*
Glendurgan (43), Mawnan Smith, *mid-Feb–Oct, Tues–Sat, and bank holidays except Good Friday*
Godolphin House (12), nr Helston, *Easter–Sep, enquire for times*
Hidden Valley (76), nr Par, *mid-Mar–Oct*
Ken-Caro (109), nr Liskeard, *end Feb–end Sep, Sun–Fri*
Lamorran House (49), St Mawes, *Apr–Sep, Wed, Fri*
Marsh Villa (83), Par, *Apr–Oct, Sun–Wed*
Mary Newman's Cottage (111), Saltash, *Easter–end Oct, Wed, Sat; groups by appointment only*
Old Mill Herbary (85), nr Bodmin, *Apr–Sep, excluding Wed*
Pencarrow (86), nr Bodmin, *Mar–Oct*
Penjerrick (52), Budock Water, *Mar–Sep, Wed–Fri and Sun, or by appointment*
Pinsla Garden (88), Cardinham, nr Bodmin, *Mar–Oct, daily*
Poldowrian (19), Coverack, *Apr–Aug, by appointment*
Potager (20), Constantine, *Apr–Sep, Suns*
Prideaux Place (90), Padstow, *Easter for 1 week, and mid-May–early Oct*
Roseland House (21), Chacewater, *Apr–Sep, Tue and Wed*
St Dellan (23), nr St Buryan, *May–Sep, not Mon, by appointment*
St Michael's Mount (24), Marazion, *May–Jun, Mon–Fri; Jul–Oct, Thu, Fri*
Tregrehan (95), nr St Austell, *mid-Mar–mid-Jun, Wed–Sun, excluding Easter;*

mid-Jun–Aug, Wed only
Trelowarren (29), Mawgan, *Apr–Sep*
Trengwainton (30), nr Penzance, *mid-Feb–end Oct, excluding Fri and Sat, but open Good Friday*
Trereife Park (31), Penzance, *Apr–Oct*
Trerice (97), nr Newquay, *end Mar–end Oct, daily excluding Sat*
Trewidden (33), nr Penzance, *Feb–Oct, Wed–Sun and bank holiday Mons*
Trewithen (65), nr Truro, *Feb–May, Mon–Sun; Jun–Sep Mon–Sat*
Trist House (66), Veryan, *Apr–Sep, Sun Tue and bank holiday Mons, and by appointment*
Wheal Darlington (36), nr Penzance, *May–Jul, by appointment*
Windman Cottage (37), nr Penzance, *May–Sep, by appointment*

3   Gardens open only occasionally

Note that the following gardens are ope only at the times stated in the Guide, ar cannot be visited at other times. On the larger estates, a charity opening does no imply any public right of way.

Gardens asterisked are also open by appointment.

January
Tregoose (94), nr Grampound

February
Tregoose (94), nr Grampound

March
Ince Castle (108), nr Saltash
Porthpean (89), nr St Austell
*Southfield (116), Poundstock
*Trevella (64), nr Truro

April
Boconnoc (68), Lostwithiel
Ince Castle (97), nr Saltash
*Hallowarren (13), Manaccan

Index

Acknowledgements

Photographs are reproduced by kind permission of: Julian Ball, p. 255; Barbara Hepworth Museum/Tate St Ives, pp. 26 (T), 27 (T, BR); John Beckett Photography, p. 195 (B); Mark Brent, p. 118; Ian Browne, p. 119; Burncoose & South Down Nurseries, pp. 32, 33 (T); James Butler, p. 101 (BR); Caerhays Castle, pp. 164–5; Ray & Shirley Clemo, pp. 196, 197; Alison Clough, p. 84; Joyce Cook, p. 132–3; Valerie Corbett, pp. 44 (T), 45; Cornwall Tourist Board, pp. 156–7; Diana Craig, p. 134; Gillian Dingle, pp. 260–61; Tim Dingle, p. 227 (T); The Eden Project, pp. 168, 169; Flambards Experience, pp. 40, 41; Bill Fry, p. 73; A. Fortescue, pp. 158–9; Gibsons of Scilly, pp. 14–15, 22 (BR), 23 (T); Michael Grose, pp. 4, 30, 31, 36, 37, 39, 64, 65, 88–93, 103, 108, 109, 112, 113, 144, 145, 162–3, 170, 171, 204, 205, 226, 227 (B), 262–5; Valerie Hadley, pp. 56, 57; Heligan Gardens, pp. 184, 185; Elizabeth Henslowe, pp. 250, 251; Jean Hill, pp. 172, 173; Alison Hodge, pp. 11 (B), 24–25, 53 (BL, BR), 70, 71, 96, 97 (T), 131 (BL, BR), 280; James Hodge, pp. 1, 2, 11 (R), 21 (B), 33 (B), 100, 117, 120, 131 (T), 118, 119 (B), 200 (T),

238, 254, 267; G.J. Holborow, p. 116; Sheila Holland, p. 187 (TL, TR); Rob & Stella Hore, pp. 176, 177; Robert Latham, pp. 258–9 (T); Christopher Laughton, pp. 66, 85; Freya Laughton, pp. 220–21, 234, 235 (T, BR); Tim Le Grice, pp. 80, 81; June Lethbridge, p. 21 (T); John Mann, p. 239; Mount Edgcumbe/Dick Ogilvie, pp. 248, 249; The National Trust/Andrew Besley, pp. 143 (B), 181 (T), 229 (T); The National Trust/Simon Cook, p. 78; The National Trust/Dan Flunder, pp. 55 (B), 225 (T); The National Trust/David Hastilow, p. 107; The National Trust/Jon Hicks, p. 181 (B), 223 (T), 228, 229 (B); The National Trust/David Judge, pp. 54–5; The National Trust/Tony Kent, pp. 143 (T), 217 (B); The National Trust/Dennis Madge, p. 180; The National Trust/Charles Mohun, p. 223 (B); The National Trust/Bill Newby, p. 79 (T); The National Trust/Marcus Way, p. 106; Lucie Nottingham, pp. 146, 147; Alison O'Connor, p. 210; Paradise Park, pp. 11 (M), 48–9; Pencarrow, pp. 194, 195 (T); Michael Perry, pp. 98, 99; Jeremy Peter-Hoblyn, p. 268; Charlotte Petherick, pp. 200 (B), 201; Mrs H.M. Piggott, pp. 86–7; Paddy Powell, pp. 208, 209

(B); Prideaux Place © Rosema Lauder, pp. 202, 203; Charlie ham, pp. 60, 61; B.J. Richards 236, 237; Mathew Robinson, 34, 35; Jane Rogers, p. 101 (B Roskillys, p. 63; Dawn Runna Cornwall Tourist Board, pp. 94 Joanne Schofield, p. 43; Peter Skerrett, pp. 58, 59; Harriet St pp. 178, 179 (TR); Rob Steerw p. 121; Joe Stephens, p. 44 (B Judith Stephens, p. 189 (B); Ch Taylor, p. 38; Rupert Tenison, 67; Trebah Garden Trust, pp. 137; Peregrine Twinkle Treffre p. 165 (T); Tregothnan Estate, 140, 141; Tresco Estate, pp. 5, 18 (TR), 19; Trevarno Estate, (T); Trewithen Estate, p. 151; S Ferrers Vyvyan, pp. 76, 77; R. Whurr, pp. 192, 193; Caroline liams, pp. 68, 69; James Willia p. 75; Claire Woodbine, pp. 19 199. All other photographs are the author.

The map of Boconnoc (p. 8 taken from The Parks & Garde Cornwall (Alison Hodge, 1998)

The map inside the back c is © Collins Bartholomew Ltd 2004, reproduced by permissi HarperCollins Publishers.